An Analytic Assessment of U.S. Drug Policy

AEI EVALUATIVE STUDIES
Marvin H. Kosters
Series Editor

An Analytic Assessment of U.S. Drug Policy

David Boyum
Peter Reuter

The AEI Press

Publisher for the American Enterprise Institute

WASHINGTON, D.C.

Available in the United States from the AEI Press, c/o Client Distribution Services, 193 Edwards Drive, Jackson, TN 38301. To order, call toll free: 1-800-343-4499. Distributed outside the United States by arrangement with Eurospan, 3 Henrietta Street, London WC2E 8LU, England.

Library of Congress Cataloging-in-Publication Data
Boyum, David.
    An analytic assessment of U.S. drug policy/ David Boyum and Peter Reuter.
    p. cm.
    Includes bibliographical references and index.
    ISBN 0-8447-4191-4 (pbk. : alk. paper)
    I. Drug Abuse—Government policy—United States. 2. Narcotics, Control of—United States. 3. Drug abuse—United States—Prevention. 4. Drug abuse—Treatment—Government policy—United States. I. Reuter, Peter. II. Title.

HV5825.B696 2005
362.29'1561'0973—dc22

                                        2004029541

09 08 07 06 05   1 2 3 4 5

Printed in the United States of America

Contents

Illustrations

Foreword

The AEI Evaluative Studies series consists of detailed empirical analyses of government programs and policies in action. Each study documents the history, purposes, operations, and political underpinnings of the program in question; analyzes its costs, consequences, and efficacy in achieving its goals; and presents proposals for reform. The studies are prepared by leading academic students of individual policy fields and are reviewed by scholars, agency officials, and program proponents and critics before publication.

The growth of public policy research in recent decades has been accompanied by a burgeoning of research and writing on proposed policies and those in the initial stages of implementation. Careful evaluation of the large base of existing programs and policies—many of them politically entrenched and no longer at the forefront of policy debate—has suffered from relative neglect. Within the government, program evaluation is typically limited to scrutiny of annual spending levels and of the number and composition of constituents who are served. Insufficient attention is devoted to fundamental questions: whether a program's social or economic goals are being accomplished, whether the goals are worthy and important, and whether they might be better achieved through alternative approaches.

The AEI series, directed by Marvin Kosters, aims to redress that imbalance. By examining government programs in action, it aims to direct more academic, political, and public attention to whether we are getting our money's worth from well-established programs and whether current "policy reform" agendas are indeed focused on issues with the greatest potential for improved public welfare.

CHRISTOPHER DEMUTH
President
American Enterprise Institute
for Public Policy Research

Acknowledgments

Jonathan Caulkins and Harold Pollack provided insightful comments on drafts of this study. We would also like to thank Alfred Blumstein, John Carnevale, Marvin Kosters, Kevin Murphy, Charles Murray, David Murray, Sally Satel, Tom Schelling, and Samuel Thernstrom for helpful comments.

Introduction

Illicit drugs constitute an apparently permanent item on the list of America's social problems. While these substances, and efforts to enforce their prohibition, loom especially large in the ills of urban minority communities, they also rank high among the concerns of Americans in general.

The purpose of this book is to provide a compact survey and analysis of the drug problem and the policy response to it in the United States. The first four chapters present a brief history of America's drug-control efforts, an analysis of present problems, a survey of policies that have been implemented in reaction to those problems—particularly by the federal government—and a critical look at their consequences. The fifth and final chapter reviews what has been learned about drug policy and suggests how it could be improved.

The chapters will show that most people who try illicit drugs use them only a few times and neither suffer nor cause any serious identifiable damage. And even though marijuana is by far the most widely used illicit drug, its negative consequences are dwarfed by those of other drugs. The tangible costs of the nation's drug problem are largely—but not exclusively—associated with the minority of drug users who are longstanding and heavy users of cocaine, crack, or heroin. These users, most of whom reside in urban poverty areas, account for the bulk of drug-related crime, illness, and premature death.

Fortunately, initiation rates have been very low for cocaine use since the late 1980s and fairly modest for heroin over the same period. The same cannot be said of methamphetamine, which has become a major problem in some parts of the country, nor of Ecstasy (MDMA) and other increasingly popular dance-club drugs. But methamphetamine is still much less important a health and crime problem than cocaine or heroin,

1

as are the club drugs, which characteristically bring a great deal less harm to their users.

The book will also show that American drug policy, rather than focusing on reducing demand among chronic abusers, has emphasized efforts to limit the supply of drugs through vigorous law enforcement. Yet despite the incarceration of hundreds of thousands of drug dealers and steadfast attempts to stop overseas cultivation and trafficking, drugs have become substantially cheaper, casting doubt on the effectiveness of this strategy.

Enforcement, which dominates both the budget and rhetoric of American drug policy, is not the only approach to drug control that has proved disappointing; as we will explain, there is little evidence justifying existing programs to prevent childhood and adolescent drug use. Drug Abuse Resistance Education (DARE), the only widely adopted prevention program, has been repeatedly demonstrated to be ineffective. By contrast, treatment programs, despite high dropout rates and difficulty in retaining good staff, have shown both effectiveness, as measured by reductions in crime and illness associated with their clients, and cost-effectiveness. But treatment programs, particularly those focused on criminally active heavy users, receive only modest funds. On the whole, then, there is now less reason than ever to believe that current policies are an efficient and effective response to the problem of illicit drugs.

Although the book touches on a wide range of issues, its scope is narrow in some respects. Throughout, we focus primarily on what available data and research tell us about the dynamics and consequences of drug use, and the characteristics and effectiveness of drug policy. Our approach to assessing the effectiveness of policy is chiefly economic: We consider, above all, identifiable costs and benefits. As such, we do not discuss the morality of drug use or its prohibition, issues that many Americans regard as decisive, since these are questions of values that cannot be quantified.

Nor do we explore the merits and demerits of legalizing drugs, even though legalization is perhaps the most prominent and hotly debated topic in drug policy. Our analysis takes current policy as its starting point, and the idea of repealing the nation's drug laws has no serious support within either the Democratic or Republican party. Moreover, because legalization is untested, any prediction of its effects would be highly speculative. MacCoun and Reuter (2001) provide a systematic account of the available data and develop projections of the consequences of various forms of legalization of cocaine, heroin, and marijuana, emphasizing their uncertainty. For the purposes of this book, we think it is more productive to concentrate on policy alternatives that are politically imaginable, and for which it is possible to reach more confident conclusions about likely consequences.

Finally, we do not examine the question of why people use drugs. Drug users have many and varied motivations—self-medication, pleasure-seeking, addiction, and risk-taking are just some of them. Identifying and understanding these impetuses may be important in designing specific drug prevention interventions, and in therapeutic contexts, where treatment regimens are matched to the characteristics and circumstances of individual patients. But such motivations are less relevant to policymaking, where decisions involve blunt instruments aimed at populations. Enforcement, for example, is hard to shape to specific user motivations.

The book is also limited in scope in that it considers only illicit drugs, despite the fact that the use of alcohol and tobacco leads to far more morbidity and mortality, and, in the case of alcohol, probably to more crime and violence as well. Illicit drugs are generally more prominent politically, involve a broader array of policy agencies than those used to deal with alcohol and cigarettes, and entail greater direct expenditures for control. Thus, we follow the common, if arbitrary, practice of using the term "drug" to refer only to illegal drugs such as cocaine, heroin, and marijuana, even though we recognize that alcohol is the most widely abused intoxicant and tobacco the substance with the greatest number of addicted users.

Since current policies are at least as much a legacy of past policies as they are a response to present circumstances, we begin with a short historical account of U.S. drug policy.

1

Historical Development

The prohibition of certain substances on the basis of their harmfulness to both users and others has a long history in the United States. Tobacco and alcohol were the principal targets of prohibition in the nineteenth century. Only toward the end of that century did cocaine and heroin, recent and very powerful additions to the pharmacopoeia available to physicians, come into focus (Musto 1999; Spillane 2000).

Until the early twentieth century, antidrug laws were largely state and local measures. However, growing concern that lax state and municipal laws were failing to contain narcotics addiction prompted federal legislation, most importantly the Harrison Act in 1914. On its surface, the Harrison Act appeared only to regulate the production and distribution of opium and coca derivatives, but in practice it was interpreted to preclude doctors from prescribing drugs to maintain addiction, and it ushered in a half-century of increasingly punitive antidrug laws. The act itself increased the maximum penalty specified in federal narcotics laws to five years from two. But by the end of the 1950s, federal and some state antinarcotics laws included life imprisonment and the death penalty and imposed mandatory minimum sentences for certain drug offenses. Still, the scale of enforcement was minor, as was drug use.

Until 1969, federal government action regarding illicit drugs was rather limited. Although antidrug legislation, including the Marihuana Tax Act of 1937, the Boggs Act of 1951, and the Narcotics Control Act of 1956, had been enacted with fanfare, neither federal funding nor programs were substantial. Despite the international prominence of its long-time director, Harry Anslinger, the Federal Bureau of Narcotics remained a small agency with no more than three hundred agents. Treatment was provided in two federal facilities that were adjuncts to prisons in Lexington, Kentucky, and Fort Worth, Texas.

But in 1969, faced with evidence of a growing heroin problem in many cities, President Nixon became the first president to declare a "war on drugs." The president focused initially on international controls, reflecting the belief that since the drugs originated overseas, so should the solution. As most heroin was thought to come from Turkey, Nixon pressured that nation to ban opium cultivation.[1] The Turkish government enacted such a ban in 1971 in return for U.S. provision of compensation payments to farmers, but Turkish electoral politics led to a rescinding of the ban and a good deal of congressional rhetoric about faithless allies. Even after the ban was lifted, however, tighter control by the Turkish government resulted in a sharp diminution in estimated heroin production in that country.

The other major initiative of the Nixon administration was the creation of a federally subsidized drug treatment system, built primarily around methadone, which had been developed as a heroin agonist in the early 1960s. Though the administration's rhetoric was hostile to Lyndon Johnson's "Great Society," it is often said that Nixon's presidency actually represented a high point for liberal social programs. Certainly, the claim is true for drug policy; treatment dominated federal antidrug spending from 1971 to 1975, although less because of a humane attitude toward drug users than because methadone seemed to offer a "silver bullet" for the heroin problem (Goldberg 1980; Massing 1998).

In the mid-1970s it became clear that the heroin epidemic had passed its peak, perhaps because of the success of overseas supply efforts (including the Turkish opium ban, the spraying of Mexican opium fields, and the breaking of the "French connection" trafficking route). As a result, interest in drug policy diminished at the federal level. Federal drug control expenditures declined, and both presidents Ford and Carter distanced themselves from the drug issue. Neither spoke much about it, and President Carter's endorsement of the removal of criminal penalties for possession of small amounts of marijuana for personal use had no legislative consequence. Even a substantial growth of marijuana use in high school populations— in 1978, nearly one in nine high school seniors reported having used it on a daily basis for the previous month—did not trigger a strong response from the Carter administration, though it led to the emergence of a strong parents' movement (U.S. Department of Health and Human Services, National Institute on Drug Abuse 2002).

Federal interest grew rapidly again after the election of Ronald Reagan, who early in his first term gave major speeches announcing new initiatives against drugs. This time cocaine was the primary target, although marijuana received increased attention as well, thanks in part to the growing influence of nonprofit antidrug organizations. For example, a Reagan speech at the Justice Department announcing the creation of a new set of prosecutor-led units (the Organized Crime Drug Enforcement Task Force program) was given great prominence. George H. W. Bush, then vice president, made much of his chairing of a border control committee and his leadership of the South Florida Initiative, aimed at closing down the major cocaine and marijuana smuggling routes into South Florida. Federal expenditures on drug control grew massively, from about $1.5 billion in fiscal year 1981 to $6.6 billion in fiscal year 1989. The bulk of that increase was for enforcement, especially interdiction, so that by 1989 less than 30 percent of federal expenditures went to prevention and treatment.

The growth of a visible cocaine problem, reflected in the deaths of two well-known young athletes eight days apart in 1986, energized Congress.[2] In a series of broad-scope antidrug bills, the penalties for violations of federal drug laws covering both possession and distribution were toughened significantly. Nor was this just punitive rhetoric; by creating a commission to set guidelines for sentences and setting high mandatory minimums, Congress ensured that those convicted in federal courts would serve long sentences. By 1992 the average time served for drug offenses in federal prison had risen to more than six years, up from about two years in 1980. Combined with increasingly aggressive investigative and prosecutorial efforts, these measures resulted in an extraordinary increase in the number and length of federal prison sentences served for drug offenses, from the equivalent of 4,500 cell-years in 1980 to over 85,000 cell-years in 1992, and over 135,000 cell-years in 2001.[3] While it is true that many in Congress expressed dissatisfaction with the emphasis on enforcement over prevention and treatment, they were unable to affect the budget division for some years.

In the final year of the Reagan administration, Congress passed the Anti-Drug Abuse Act of 1988. In a provision resisted by the Reagan administration, the act mandated the creation of a single organization within the

White House to manage the entire federal drug-control effort, which was seen as being in bureaucratic disarray. The Office of National Drug Control Policy (ONDCP, colloquially known as the drug czar's office) was required to present an annual strategy, along with quantifiable long-term and short-term goals.

At about this time, a sharp spike in popular concern about the drug problem briefly made it the leading national issue in polls. President George H. W. Bush made drugs the subject of his first prime-time televised address in September 1989. ONDCP's first director, William Bennett (appointed by President Bush), provided a clear rationale for the focus on criminal penalties. The problem, said Bennett, was drug use itself, rather than its consequences; in this he departed from a number of earlier statements associated with the Carter and Ford administrations. Success was to be measured not by reductions in crime or disease associated with drugs, but in the numbers of users (U.S. Office of National Drug Control Policy 1989). Bennett's successor, former Florida governor Bob Martinez, made little impact on the course of federal policy, which was dominated by funding for enforcement agencies such as the Customs Service and the Coast Guard. The share of the growing federal drug-control budget ($13 billion in fiscal year 1992) going to prevention and treatment rose very slowly during the Bush administration.

The Clinton administration efforts can readily be summarized: no change (Carnevale and Murphy 1999). There were some differences in rhetoric, with greater emphasis on the small number of offenders who were frequent drug users. However, that had no material impact on the allocation of the federal drug-control budget; two-thirds continued to go to enforcement activities, predominantly inside the United States. Sentencing policy did not change, either; large numbers of federal defendants continued to receive and serve long prison sentences for drug offenses. Between 1992 and 2000, the number of federal prisoners serving time for drug offenses rose from 35,398 to 63,898 (U.S. Department of Justice, Bureau of Justice Statistics 2003a).

The administration of George W. Bush has made changes in both substance and rhetoric. Internationally, much less emphasis has been placed on blaming Latin America for the inflow of drugs. Meeting with Mexican president Vicente Fox in February 2001, President Bush said, "One of the reasons why drugs are shipped—the main reason why drugs are shipped through Mexico to the United States is because United States citizens use drugs. And our nation must do a better job of educating our citizenry about the dangers and evils of drug use. Secondly, I believe there is a movement in the country to review all the certification process" (Office of the Press Secretary 2001).[4] As a consequence, the annual fight about certification of the drug control efforts by Mexico, often the source of great indignation there, subsided.

At the same time, there was increasing emphasis on the dangers of marijuana. ONDCP published many documents making the case that marijuana was more dangerous than generally perceived by adults, and certainly more dangerous than it was twenty years ago when it had a lower THC content. ONDCP Director John Walters was also harshly critical of Canada's decision to remove criminal penalties for possession of small amounts of marijuana, even though this was consistent with the policy of at least eleven U.S. states. "You expect your friends to stop the movement of poison to your neighborhood. And that is what's going on here. If we were sending toxic substances to your young people, you would be and should be upset" (Harper 2003).

It is hard to describe how the Bush administration has changed drug control expenditures. As will be noted in chapter 3, ONDCP has altered what counts as enforcement expenditures for budgetary purposes. Rhetoric has emphasized both prevention and treatment, with the president making a number of statements about the importance of having an adequate number of treatment slots available. The most visible of the administration's drug policy efforts is the National Youth Anti-Drug Media Campaign, launched in 1998 during the Clinton administration, which has placed extensive paid and donated antidrug advertising on television and radio, in print media, and on the Internet. It remains to be seen if support for the media campaign wanes, since evaluations sponsored by the National Institute on Drug Abuse have consistently cast doubt on the efficacy of the campaign messages (U.S. Department of Health and Human Services, National Institute on Drug Abuse 2003).

State and Local Policy

Though state and local governments may play a larger role in drug control than the federal government, it is much more difficult to provide a capsule history of drug control at state and local levels. There was a brief period during which state and some city governments followed the federal lead and created drug-czar-like agencies, but that faded. Authority now tends to be dispersed, with a large array of agencies having substantial roles, but few specializing in dealing with drugs.

One consequence is that data about state and local antidrug activities are rather limited. For instance, drug convictions result from arrests by local police and the actions of county prosecutors. However, apart from raw counts of arrests and convictions, there is no systematic information about the size or shape of state and local enforcement of drug laws around the nation.

Nonetheless, it seems likely that the main story line of state and local policy is even simpler than at the federal level. Legislatures have enacted progressively tougher statutes, criminalizing more drug-related activities and imposing steadily increasing penalties for those convicted. The net effect has been enormous: In 1980, fewer than 20,000 drug offenders were incarcerated in state facilities; by 2000, over 250,000 drug offenders were in state custody—a trend that only very recently has shown signs of slowing. (We take up this change in the final chapter.) States and cities have been unwilling to spend their own funds on prevention or treatment; as we shall see later, these are heavily funded by the federal government, even though it is hard to provide a federalism argument that they are more worthy of federal support than enforcement.

Objectives of U.S. Drug Policy

Any assessment of U.S. drug policy must consider its stated objectives, for if that policy is a heritage of historical efforts at drug control, it is also a product of a particular conception of what drug policy should try to accomplish. These goals, although widely accepted, are problematic; some of the failures of current policies may be as much the consequence of inadequate or misguided goals as of approaches to achieving them.

At least since 1989, when the first National Drug Control Strategy was submitted to Congress by the Bush administration, the principal goal of federal drug policy has been to reduce the number of users. "[T]he highest priority of our drug policy," wrote ONDCP Director Bennett, "must be a stubborn determination further to reduce the overall level of drug use nationwide—experimental first use, 'casual' use, regular use and addiction alike" (U.S. Office of National Drug Control Policy 1989, 8). In other words, the leading goal was to reduce the percentage of Americans who used drugs, quantities commonly referred to as the *prevalence* of drug use. Although the National Drug Control Strategies produced by the Clinton administration placed less emphasis on reducing overall prevalence and called more attention to the problem of chronic drug abuse, there was, as noted earlier, little identifiable change in policy. The administration of George W. Bush still emphasizes use reduction.

An overriding goal of reducing the number of drug users favors some programs over others (Caulkins and Reuter 1997). Enforcement and primary prevention, which represent broad-based efforts to discourage drug use, look attractive if prevalence reduction is the main objective of drug policy. Treatment programs, which target the addicted, are less appealing. Chronic drug abusers are few in number compared with casual users, and treatment programs are far more effective at tempering the drug habits and criminal activity of heavy users than at helping them attain abstinence.

Least effective from the perspective of prevalence reduction are secondary and tertiary prevention efforts that seek to reduce the damage caused by drug use rather than limit drug use itself. This helps explain why needle exchange has never been supported by ONDCP,[5] and why methadone maintenance, whose purpose is to replace a more damaging drug habit with a less damaging one, remains somewhat controversial despite its amply documented success in reducing the problems of heroin addicts.[6] The overriding focus on prevalence also helps to explain why marijuana, the most widely used illicit drug, attracts so much attention from drug policymakers, even though its contribution to crime and violence, relative to cocaine and heroin, is minor, as probably is its contribution to mortality and morbidity.

The data presented in the next chapter will demonstrate the main problem with a drug policy that sets its sights on overall prevalence: Most of the damage associated with drugs involves a small minority of drug users who engage in compulsive use, and it is not clear that rates of heavy use are affected much by overall prevalence, except perhaps in the long run. Over time, prevalence may influence the number of casual users who become the next generation of heavy users, but because long-term abstinence comes slowly, if at all, to most chronic users (Hser et al. 2001), turnover in the heavy user population is remarkably slow. Thus, even a substantial reduction in levels of occasional use will do little to lower the number of heavy users in the next few years.

Supply Reduction vs. Demand Reduction

The history of American drug policy can be viewed as a longstanding dispute over whether drug abuse is best dealt with as a criminal or medical problem (Musto 1999). In policymaking, this debate manifests itself in the division of programs into "supply reduction" and "demand reduction," and endless battling over the funding of the two categories. For practical purposes, supply reduction means drug enforcement, and demand reduction means drug treatment. While prevention is often considered demand reduction, it does not factor into the cops-versus-docs debate, since everyone supports the concept of prevention.

Supply reduction and demand reduction are not necessarily dichotomous. For example, drug enforcement can lead addicts to treatment, either directly, when arrested addicts are compelled into treatment by the judicial system, or indirectly, when by making it difficult, expensive, and risky to buy drugs, enforcement makes treatment appear more attractive to addicts than continued use. But such connections between enforcement and treatment occur mainly at state and local levels of government. Federal drug enforcement is targeted at high-level traffickers; the link to the treatment of addicts is distant. Consequently, the allocation of resources to supply- and demand-reduction activities is a reasonable measure of policy emphasis at the federal level.

That said, the framing of drug policy as supply reduction versus demand reduction can easily be misleading. Consider that drug enforcement, or supply reduction, lessens the use and abuse of drugs, an important public health goal. And note that the principal effect of drug treatment, the main demand-reduction program, is to decrease crime, the central objective of law enforcement. Is supply reduction a public health program and demand reduction a law enforcement program?

Despite the murkiness of the terms, supply reduction and demand reduction have become accepted parlance, and supply and demand are important concepts for analyzing drug use and connecting policy interventions to outcomes. Illicit drugs are, after all, products that are bought and sold in markets, and consumption of them is thus influenced by the interaction of supply and demand. Drug policy can reduce consumption by making it more difficult and risky to produce, distribute, and sell drugs (supply reduction), and by lowering people's desire and ability to purchase drugs (demand reduction). This is the basic economic framework that underlies our analysis.

2

America's Drug Problems

Overview

This chapter provides a description of recent developments in Americans' use of drugs and its consequences. The first part of the story is easily summarized. About one in fifteen Americans ages twelve and over currently uses drugs. By a wide margin, prevalence is highest among older teenagers and those in their early twenties, peaking at around 40 percent use within the past twelve months for high school seniors. Most Americans who try drugs use them only a few times. If there is a typical continuing user, it is an occasional marijuana smoker who will cease to use drugs at some point during his twenties. Marijuana use for the fifteen- to twenty-six-year-old age group has been at high levels throughout the past three decades, but there have also been notable ups and downs. Usage rose through the 1970s, fell in the 1980s, and bounced back up in the early 1990s, particularly among adolescents.[1]

While most drug users at any given time are occasional marijuana smokers, a substantial (and, on average, older) minority are chronic abusers of heroin, cocaine, and crack. These long-term users together account for the greater part of the volume of overall drug consumption, as measured in expenditures. They are largely the product of the three drug epidemics the nation has experienced since the late 1960s, the first involving heroin, the second cocaine powder, and the third crack. Whether methamphetamine or Ecstasy will generate a fourth national epidemic, leaving a large population of impaired or dependent users, remains to be seen.

The second part of the story, regarding the consequences of drug use and control, is much more complicated. Statistics show that much crime, both property and violent, and a substantial amount of disease, is associated with drug use, particularly dependence. However, causal attribution is difficult. The behavioral problems of the drug-dependent are often inchoate prior to drug use, and the substantial worsening of these problems that accompanies use is at least partly the consequence of policies that marginalize users and make habits costly to support, and not simply an effect of the drugs themselves.

Drug Use

Patterns of Use. Drug use by Americans is primarily measured by two surveys: the National Survey on Drug Use and Health (NSDUH), formerly called the National Household Survey on Drug Abuse, and Monitoring the Future (MTF). The NSDUH, which samples residents, ages twelve and older, of known household addresses, and MTF, which covers high school students, have tracked drug use in the general population since the mid-1970s. Consistent with a main policy goal of reducing prevalence, these surveys are used to estimate the numbers and percentages of Americans of different ages who have used and currently use drugs. They include questions about the quantities of drugs used, but these data are unreliable and rarely reported or analyzed.

The NSDUH and MTF do a better job of identifying patterns and trends in occasional rather than heavy drug use, especially for cocaine, crack, and heroin. Heavy users of cocaine, crack, and heroin are often socially isolated and thus beyond the reach of general population surveys. But given the prominence of the NSDUH and MTF, these surveys provide a useful starting point in looking at American drug use.

Table 2-1 summarizes findings from the 2003 NSDUH. Shown are the numbers and percentages of Americans in different age categories estimated to have used various illicit drugs in the past month.

The data indicate that marijuana is, by a wide margin, the most commonly used illicit drug. Three-quarters of users report using marijuana (14.6 million out of a total of 19.5 million users), while fewer than half report use of any other illicit drug (8.8 million of 19.5 million). The data also suggest that drug-use rates drop sharply after young adulthood. In

TABLE 2-1

ESTIMATED NUMBER (IN MILLIONS) AND PERCENTAGE OF PAST-MONTH
DRUG USERS AMONG PERSONS AGES TWELVE AND OVER, 2003

Drug	Ages 12 and over		Ages 12–17		Ages 18–25		Ages 26 and over	
Any Illicit Drug	19.5	8.2%	2.8	11.2%	6.4	20.3%	10.2	5.6%
Marijuana and Hashish	14.6	6.2%	2.0	7.9%	5.4	17.0%	7.3	4.0%
Cocaine and Crack	2.3	1.0%	0.2	0.6%	0.7	2.2%	1.4	0.8%
Heroin	0.1	0.1%	0.0	0.1%	0.0	0.1%	0.1	0.0%
Hallucinogens	1.0	0.4%	0.3	1.0%	0.5	1.7%	0.2	0.1%
Inhalants	0.6	0.2%	0.3	1.3%	0.1	0.4%	0.1	0.1%
Nonmedical Use of Prescription Drugs	6.3	2.7%	1.0	4.0%	1.9	6.0%	3.4	1.9%
Any Illicit Drug Other Than Marijuana	8.8	3.7%	1.4	5.7%	2.7	8.4%	4.8	2.6%

SOURCE: U.S. Department of Health and Human Services, Substance Abuse and Mental Health Services Administration 2004a.

fact, NSDUH figures may understate this decline in the case of cocaine, crack, and heroin, since the over-twenty-five age group includes large and aging cohorts who initiated use of these drugs in the 1970s and 1980s.

Figure 2-1 shows the percentages of high school seniors who reported using any illicit drug in the past year from 1975 to 2003, and the percentages of those ages twelve to seventeen and eighteen to twenty-five who reported past-year use. Data on high school seniors are taken from the MTF; age-group data are drawn from the NSDUH and its predecessor.[2]

For the most part, the surveys tell a consistent story. The prevalence of drug use among younger Americans peaked around 1979, declined until 1992, rebounded somewhat over the next five years, and then leveled off. (The rise from 2001 to 2002 shown by the NSDUH—but not by MTF—is likely the result of changes in the methodology of the NSDUH survey designed to improve the accuracy of reporting.[3]) This pattern is politically convenient for Republicans, some of whom have noted that drug use rose during the Carter and Clinton presidencies and dropped substantially during the Reagan and George H. W. Bush administrations. But it is hard to identify policy changes that might have led to the turning

FIGURE 2-1
PAST-YEAR DRUG USE, 1975–2003

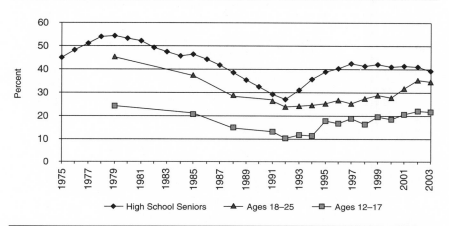

SOURCE: U.S. Department of Health and Human Services, Substance Abuse and Mental Health Services Administration 1999, 2001b, 2002d, 2004a; U.S. Department of Health and Human Services, National Institute on Drug Abuse 2004.

points. Moreover, note that the figures estimate only the percentages of individuals who used drugs, not the volume, severity, or effects of drug use. Because approximately half of users in the NSDUH and MTF reported using only marijuana, prevalence figures are heavily driven by marijuana use. Figure 2-1 shows overall drug use declining significantly during the 1980s, precisely when crack use soared.

The accuracy of the NSDUH and MTF data is also a matter of debate. The surveys rely on self-reporting of an illegal activity by household residents and high school students. Some respondents give false answers, and the false response rate varies over time with attitudes toward the acceptability of drug use. More important, those who use drugs most frequently— and may have become school dropouts, homeless, or otherwise socially marginalized—are particularly hard to reach in such surveys. That said, the surveys probably capture the general trends in occasional drug use, with some exaggeration in the speed of upturns and downturns. When drug use is increasing (and thus less widely disapproved of by the relevant population groups), users tend to be more willing to report their use. Correspondingly, downturns in drug use are likely to be accompanied by

TABLE 2-2

PERCENTAGE OF ADULT MALE ARRESTEES TESTING
POSITIVE FOR DRUGS IN SEVEN MAJOR CITIES, 2003

Primary City	Any NIDA-5 Drug[a]	Marijuana	Cocaine/ Crack	Opiates	Metham- phetamine
Chicago, IL	86.0	53.2	50.6	24.9	1.4
Dallas, TX	62.3	39.1	32.7	6.9	5.8
Los Angeles, CA	68.6	40.7	23.5	2.0	28.7
New York, NY	69.7	43.1	35.7	15.0	0.0
Philadelphia, PA	67.0	45.8	30.3	11.5	0.6
Phoenix, AZ	74.1	40.9	23.4	4.4	38.3
San Diego, CA	66.8	41.0	10.3	5.1	36.2
Median (39 cities)	67.0	44.1	30.1	5.8	4.7

SOURCE: U.S. Department of Justice, National Institute of Justice 2004.
a. The NIDA-5 drugs are cocaine, opiates, marijuana, methamphetamine, and PCP.

reduced willingness to report. Turning points are probably identified with reasonable accuracy.

The surveys do much less well in describing trends in use by people dependent on drugs, at least for expensive and debilitating drugs such as cocaine and heroin. There are at least three reasons: Dependent users are, first, much less likely to respond to these surveys because they lead more erratic lives; second, less likely to provide truthful responses to survey questions; and third, more likely to be found among nonhousehold populations, such as the homeless and the incarcerated.[4] The federal government did not produce official estimates of the size of the heroin-addicted population for almost twenty years (from the mid-1970s to the early 1990s) and in doing so recently has relied primarily on data sources other than the NSDUH. The NSDUH generates an estimate of 1.2 million for all past-month cocaine users, while other official estimates, using a greater variety of sources, indicate about 2 million who used at least eight times in the previous month (U.S. Office of National Drug Control Policy 2000).

The NSDUH and MTF surveys have been complemented by the Arrestee Drug Abuse Monitoring program (ADAM), which until recently administered urinalyses and questionnaires to samples of people arrested in thirty-nine cities.[5] Table 2-2 shows the percentages of adult male arrestees who tested positive in ADAM-administered urinalyses in the seven largest of those cities during 2003.

Arrestees show much higher rates of drug use than the general household population, particularly for drugs other than marijuana. Equally significant, ADAM questionnaire data confirm the widely held belief that criminally active users are typically higher-volume consumers than those who report drug use in the NSDUH and MTF. Indeed, Mark Kleiman (1997) has argued that these differences are so great that arrestees and those under the supervision of the criminal justice system as parolees or probationers account for most of the nation's cocaine and heroin consumption in volume terms.

There is an important general pattern here. The use of most drugs is quite skewed: A modest fraction of all users accounts for a large share of total consumption. That is true for alcohol.[6] For marijuana, cocaine, and crack cocaine, a reasonable guess is that 20 percent of all users may account for 80 percent of the quantity consumed. This is not the case for heroin, as the aging cohorts of addicted users dominate the user population in number. Consequently, it may be that something closer to one-half of heroin users accounts for 80 percent of heroin consumption.

The urinalysis results presented in table 2-2 also demonstrate that patterns of heavy drug use have an important local element. Cities with high levels of use among arrestees for one drug often have low rates for others. Chicago, for instance, has the second-highest rate of opiate positives (24.9 percent) of cities in the ADAM program, but shows virtually no methamphetamine use. By contrast, Phoenix has one of the lowest positive rate for opiates (4.4 percent) and one of the highest for methamphetamine (38.3 percent).

It appears that drugs other than cocaine, heroin, and marijuana are widely used only in certain places or for limited periods of time in the United States, although Ecstasy may have become a long-term component of youth culture across the nation.[7] For example, in 1987, PCP (phencyclidine, a hallucinogen) was found in the urine of about half of all arrestees in Washington, D.C.; in Baltimore, just thirty-five miles away, the figure was less than 5 percent. The fraction in Washington then dropped rapidly and has remained below 10 percent since 1990.[8] Methamphetamine use is prevalent in Phoenix, San Diego, and several other cities, but rare in the rest of the country; for many years, most of the deaths related to methamphetamine were found in just five cities.[9] In recent years, there have been sharp upsurges in the fraction of arrestees testing positive for methamphetamine in a number of western and midwestern cities, generating concern about a new national epidemic in the use of a cheap stimulant. But so far, the epidemic seems to have stopped at the Mississippi River, with rates in eastern cities remaining near zero. Rates are also very low in some major western cities such as Dallas and Denver.

It is unclear why, in an age of mass communication and easy domestic transport, drug use is often a local or regional phenomenon more than a national one. Although the geographic patterns of drug use are interesting and potentially important for policy formulation, there has been little research on the issue. Nevertheless, the great local and regional variations seem to underscore the unpredictable, fad-like nature of much drug use, as well as the importance of local and regional tailoring in federally driven policies.

Prior to drug testing of arrestees, the most commonly cited data on heavy drug use came from the Drug Abuse Warning Network (DAWN), which gives estimates of the numbers of drug-related emergency department (ED) visits and deaths in most major cities. Both components of DAWN have fundamental measurement problems (Caulkins and Ebener 1995), and it is especially important to recognize that DAWN data include more than overdoses and unexpected reactions to drugs. DAWN also counts as "drug-related" ED visits and deaths related to chronic conditions brought on by drug use, even if there is no indication of current use. Nonetheless, the relentless rise in cocaine- and heroin-related deaths and ED visits, as indicated in figure 2-2, is hard to explain as a mere artifact of weak data systems. At a minimum, the data suggest that the general health status of cocaine and heroin addicts is worsening, even if their numbers are not rising.[10] The marijuana figures are somewhat misleading, since most of the admissions involve other, more dangerous drugs as well. The share that involves marijuana alone is approximately 20 percent.

Drug use data systems have improved over the last decade, particularly the NSDUH and ADAM. Still, they provide only rough approximations of the extent of drug dependence, as exemplified by a recent official series that includes estimates of the number of heroin addicts in the country (U.S. Office of National Drug Control Policy 2000, 2001a). Relying on National

FIGURE 2-2
DAWN EMERGENCY DEPARTMENT MENTIONS, 1994–2002

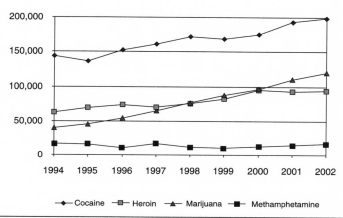

SOURCE: U.S. Department of Health and Human Services, Substance Abuse and Mental Health Services Administration 2002a, 2003.

Household Survey and ADAM data, a 2000 report from this series showed a decline of nearly one-third in the number of "hard-core" heroin users between 1988 and 1992, followed by a 56 percent increase from 1992 to 1998. In an update less than two years later, the 1988–1992 estimates were revised upwards by more than 40 percent, and the figures indicated a *decline* in the number of hardcore users after 1992. While it is plausible to say, as these official estimates do, that in recent years about 1 million people outside of prison have been active heroin addicts, the true figure might be anywhere from 500,000 to 2 million. For cocaine the number is probably twice as high, but similarly imprecise.

Note that these numbers are small compared to the roughly 20 million estimated to have used an illicit drug in the past month, according to the population surveys. Experimentation with drugs is a common experience among adolescents (Kandel 1993; Shedler and Block 1990). For most birth cohorts since 1960, over half have tried an illicit drug, marijuana being by far the most common. Without marijuana, the figure drops dramatically but still leaves a substantial minority with at least some experimental experience. For example, 28.7 percent of high school seniors in 2004 reported having tried some illicit drug other than mari-juana. The birth cohorts coming to maturity in the late 1970s were much more involved with drugs than any others. As noted earlier, the prevalence of drug use dropped sharply in the late 1980s, rose substantially and steadily in the early 1990s, and then flattened out. Much attention has been given to the rise in marijuana use among adolescents, which has indeed increased alarmingly, but that has been accompanied by shorter using-careers among adults.[11]

Desistance. Most who start using illicit drugs desist of their own volition, without treatment or coercion, within five years of initiation.[12] Indeed, even by twelfth grade, over 60 percent of those who admit to having been daily users of marijuana also report having cut back from that usage rate.[13] Few who try illicit drugs, even a number of times, become dependent users.[14] This represents a very different pattern from that for the legally available psychoactive drugs, alcohol and cigarettes. Most who use alcohol and tobacco, even occasionally, have lengthy using-careers, measured in terms of decades. Cigarette smokers consume quite heavily (over half consume at least fifteen cigarettes per day) throughout most of their careers, although the proportion of light smokers has been increasing (Okuyemi et al. 2002). Legal availability may have a separate effect on career length as well as on initiation.

Desistance from occasional use of harder drugs seems to be strongly associated with education; those who have continued to be frequent cocaine users, for instance, are less educated and more criminally active. Cocaine and crack dependence is highly concentrated in inner-city minority communities.

Marijuana dependence is more prevalent than dependence on either cocaine or heroin. A few million Americans smoke marijuana daily, indeed, several times each day. There is little research, however, about these users, and only a very small fraction of them seeks treatment. It seems that although most of them would like to quit and have been unable to do so, their dependence does not produce great damage to themselves or others (Kleiman 1992, chapter 9; Hall and Pacula 2003).

Drug Epidemics. The notion of a drug epidemic captures the fact that drug use is a learned behavior, transmitted from one person to another. Contrary to the popular image of the entrepreneurial "drug pusher" who hooks new addicts through aggressive salesmanship,[15] it is now clear that almost all first experiences are the result of being offered the drug by a friend. Drug use thus spreads much like a communicable disease; users are "contagious," and some of those with whom they come into contact become "infected." Initiation of heroin, cocaine, and crack use shows much more of a classic epidemic pattern than marijuana, although the growth of marijuana use in the 1960s may have had epidemic features. Jonathan Caulkins has collaborated with a number of other researchers to produce a series of elegant models assessing the relationship among epidemics of use, the population of frequent drug users, and various policy instruments (see, for example, Caulkins 2001).

In an epidemic, rates of initiation (infection) in a given area rise sharply as new and highly contagious users of a drug initiate friends and peers (Hunt and Chambers 1976; Rydell and Everingham 1994). At least with heroin, cocaine, and crack, long-term addicts are not particularly contagious. They are more socially isolated than new users and, knowing the pitfalls of prolonged use, may not want to expose others. Moreover, they usually present an unappealing picture of the consequences of addiction. In the next stage of the epidemic, initiation declines rapidly as the susceptible population shrinks, both because there are fewer nonusers and because some nonusers have developed "immunity," the result of better knowledge of the effects of a drug.

In the past thirty-five years, there have been three major drug epidemics, each of which has left a legacy of users with long-term problems. The first involved heroin and developed with rapid initiation in the late 1960s, primarily in a few big cities, and heavily in inner-city minority communities; the experiences of a large number of American soldiers in Vietnam may have been a contributing factor. By 1975 the number of new heroin initiates had dropped significantly (Kozel and Adams 1986), perhaps because the negative consequences of regular heroin use had become so conspicuous in those communities. In an early 1990s sample of street heroin addicts, Ann-Marie Rocheleau and David Boyum also found evidence of much higher initiation rates in the early 1970s than in the following two decades (U.S. Office of National Drug Control Policy 1994a).

Heroin initiation may have risen again in the late 1990s, but the indicators are ambiguous.[16] The possibility of a new epidemic is troubling, since heroin addiction (at least for those addicted in the United States rather than while in the military in Vietnam) has turned out to be a long-lived and lethal condition, as revealed in a remarkable thirty-three-year follow-up of male heroin addicts admitted to the California Civil Addict Program (CAP) during the years 1962–64. Nearly half of the original addicts—284 of 581—had died by 1996–97; of the 242 still living who were interviewed, 40 percent reported heroin use in the past year, and 60 percent were unemployed (Hser et al. 2001).

Cocaine, in powder form, was the source of the second epidemic, which lasted longer and was less sharply peaked than the heroin epidemic. Initiation, which was broadly distributed across class and race, rose in the late 1970s and early 1980s and then declined after about 1985 (U.S. Department of Justice, National Institute of Justice 1997). Dependence became prevalent in the mid-1980s, as the pool of those who had experimented with the drug expanded. The number of dependent users peaked around 1988 and declined only moderately through the 1990s. Whether dependence on a stimulant can be maintained as long as narcotic dependence is unclear, but there are certainly many cocaine users who have, over a ten-year period, maintained frequent use of the drug, albeit with less regularity than heroin addicts.

The third epidemic was of crack use. Although connected to the cocaine epidemic—crack developed as a cheap and easy-to-use form of freebase cocaine (Courtwright 1995)—the crack epidemic was sharper and shorter, and more concentrated among minorities in inner-city communities. Its starting point varied across cities; for Los Angeles the beginning may have been 1982, while for Chicago it was as late as 1988. But in all cities initiation appears to have peaked within about two years and to have again left a population with a chronic and debilitating addiction.

An important characteristic of a drug epidemic is that the distribution of use changes over its course. In the early stages there are many occasional users and few who are as yet dependent. As the epidemic of new use comes to an end, many light users desist, while a few go on to become frequent and dependent users. Thus, the number of users may decrease even as the total quantity of drugs consumed goes up. This is precisely the finding of Rydell and Everingham (1994) with respect to cocaine. The number of cocaine users declined sharply after about 1982, but because of the contemporaneous growth in the number of frequent users, total consumption continued to rise until 1988 at least, and declined only slowly after that.[17]

The Gateway Effect. In part, the great concern about marijuana use reflects its possible role as a "gateway" to use of more dangerous drugs. In the National Household Survey, 98 percent of users of cocaine and heroin report that they had used marijuana before initiating use of these hard drugs (Golub and Johnson 2001). Those who have used marijuana are far more likely to use hard drugs than those who have not—a widely cited figure is that a youthful marijuana user is eighty-five times more likely to use cocaine than an eighteen-year-old who has not used marijuana (Center on Addiction and Substance Abuse 1994). And the greater the frequency of an adolescent's marijuana use, the higher the chance that he or she will initiate hard drug use (Ellickson, Hays, and Bell 1992; Fergusson and Horwood 1997, 2000).

But while marijuana initiation and use are clearly associated with subsequent use of hard drugs, the existence and magnitude of any causal connection are uncertain. The key questions are: To what extent does marijuana use itself lead to cocaine and heroin use? And, alternatively, to what degree are marijuana, cocaine, and heroin use common responses to individual and environmental factors that increase the propensity to use all drugs?

A New Zealand longitudinal study (Fergusson and Horwood 2000) found evidence of a very large increase in the probability of using hard drugs depending on use of marijuana, even after attempting to control for other suspected risk factors. However, in a recent paper, Morral, McCaffrey, and Paddock (2002) showed that the observed gateway effect could nonetheless be explained simply by differences in individual propensities and opportunities to use drugs. Perhaps the best effort to control for such differences is an Australian study that looked at 311 pairs of same-sex twins—136 identical-twin pairs and 175 fraternal pairs—in which only one twin had used marijuana by age seventeen (Lynskey et al. 2003). The researchers found that despite the substantial overlap in genes and environment, the early marijuana users were about four times more likely to use cocaine and opiates when compared to their twins. Since there were still genetic, environmental, and developmental differences between twins that the study could not take into account—such as twins having dissimilar proclivities for delinquency, or attending different schools—this result might be considered an upper limit on any causal gateway effect.

The gateway effect has many interpretations. MacCoun (1998a) identifies seven, representing a wide range of causal effects. For example, the gateway effect may be the consequence of marijuana use increasing the taste for other intoxicants, an effect of the drug itself. But it could also be the product of the illegality of marijuana and other drugs; having learned how to acquire marijuana from dealers, the user now has contact with those who sell cocaine and heroin as well. It is likely that a number of mechanisms operate simultaneously at the population level. Some users do want to try stronger intoxicants, and some do come into contact with dealers who make it easier to gain access to other illegal drugs. Assessing the relative importance of each effect is impossible at the moment.

There is reason to suppose that the gateway effect varies over time and is less pronounced than it used to be. Of National Household Survey respondents born in 1962–63 (a peak use cohort) who reported using marijuana before age eighteen, 39 percent had gone on to use cocaine or heroin by age twenty-six (Golub and Johnson 2001). (Few start on the harder drugs after that age.) After that cohort, the probability of transition from marijuana to the harder drugs declined sharply. It fell to 24 percent for the 1970–71 cohort, and appears to be even lower among cohorts that have come of age more recently. This explains why the increase in adolescent marijuana use during the 1990s did not produce, as many feared it would, a subsequent surge in hard drug use.

Consequences of Drug Use

Survey data on the number and percentage of Americans who have recently used illegal drugs dominate official discussions of the drug problem. For example, in profiling America's drug use, the National Drug Control Strategy leads off by presenting an estimate of the total number of past-month drug users and comparing that prevalence rate to earlier years. But prevalence estimates, while important, say little about the negative consequences of drug use, such as the societal cost of lost productivity, health care, and crime attributable to drugs. Indeed, trends in the numbers of users can easily move in the opposite direction to trends in drug-related damage. From about 1980 to 1988, fewer and fewer Americans used illegal drugs, as illustrated in figure 2-1 above. But because of the spread of crack and HIV during that period, the identifiable harm associated with drug use rose enormously. Emergency department mentions for cocaine, for example, increased by more than a factor of ten during the 1980s, from 7,712 in 1980 to 110,013 in 1989 (U.S. Office of National Drug Control Policy 2002a).

Recognizing that all drug use is potentially hazardous does not imply that all is equally risky. Most drug use does not lead to identifiable harm, as even William Bennett noted in his introduction to the first National Drug Control Strategy; some drug use leads to staggering damage—to users themselves, to their families, and to the victims of their crimes. Moreover, while these outcomes are somewhat unpredictable in individual cases, they are far from random. It is possible to identify which types of users of which drugs are most likely to generate harm.

The drug problem should be measured at least in part, then, in terms of identifiable consequences, and not simply the numbers of users, though use can certainly be counted as one of the adverse consequences. Doing so requires an understanding of which aspects of the drug problem are most damaging. We summarize here what is known about the contribution of illicit drugs (mostly cocaine and heroin) to crime, disease, and lost productivity.

Drugs and Crime. Active criminals are far more likely than others to be drug users, as indicated by the results of the ADAM urine tests reported in table 2-2 above. In every major city, more than half of arrestees test positive for drugs (U.S. Department of Justice, National Institute of Justice 2004). Surveys of inmates in correctional institutions also show high rates of use among criminals. In 1997, 33 percent of state prisoners and 22 percent of federal prisoners reported being under the influence of drugs at the time of their current offense (U.S. Department of Justice, Bureau of Justice Statistics 1999).

While these figures do not by themselves prove that drug use causes crime, they are certainly suggestive, and there is other evidence demonstrating that drug use intensifies criminal activity. Criminally active users typically commit offenses several times as frequently during periods of heavy use as during periods of abstinence (Ball et al. 1981).

Drugs can lead to crime through a variety of mechanisms (U.S. Department of Justice, National Institute of Justice 2003). Intoxication and addiction can induce violent behavior or otherwise lead to crime by weakening judgment and self-control. Users commit crimes to obtain drug money, in part because their habits reduce opportunities for legitimate work. Drug markets—and particularly open drug markets—contribute to homicides and other violent crime, partly as a result of competition among dealers, but also because of gun acquisition related to dealing (Cork 1999). Drug selling also involves hurried transactions without documents to back up uncertain memories and has no civil justice system to peacefully resolve the resulting disputes among a population with weak self-control. Lastly, involvement in drug use and drug selling can change people's lifestyles and social ties in various ways that make criminal activity more likely.

The links between drugs and crime differ across drugs. Although some 40 percent of arrestees test positive for marijuana nationwide, it is widely accepted that marijuana is not responsible for as much crime as cocaine or heroin. Marijuana does not appear to have aggression-inducing pharmacological properties. Marijuana habits are less expensive to support than cocaine or heroin habits. And marijuana is bought and sold in markets that, while not free of violence, are less violent than cocaine and heroin markets, perhaps because so much is sold in residential settings—for instance, college dormitories—by dealers who do not themselves have expensive habits.

In contrast to marijuana, cocaine is an expensive and potentially aggression-inducing drug that is distributed in violent markets. Heroin is less often tied to violence than cocaine, but because of the persistence of heroin addiction and the more regular use of the drug, it is possible that heroin addicts typically commit more income-generating crimes over time than cocaine addicts. It is worth noting that more crimes—and in particular, more violent crimes—are committed under the influence of alcohol than under the influence of all illegal drugs combined (U.S. Department of Justice, Bureau of Justice Statistics 1999).

The research on violence in the cocaine markets was mostly conducted in the 1980s and very early 1990s. At that stage, cocaine markets, particularly those for crack, were populated mainly by users in their teens and early twenties, who were then early in their addiction careers. As these users and dealers have aged and have not been fully replaced by younger users and dealers, these markets appear to have become less violent. Thus, the reported difference between the cocaine and heroin markets may have had less to do with the characteristics of the drugs than with the age of partici-pants at the time of research.

What share of violence can be blamed on drugs is anybody's guess. Countless other factors contribute to violence, and so whether drugs or something else played the decisive role in a violent incident is a highly subjective judgment. In 1988, Paul Goldstein and several colleagues esti-mated that 52.7 percent of New York City's homicides were drug-related (Goldstein et al. 1989). Around the same time, Carolyn and Richard Block investigated 288 gang-motivated homicides in Chicago, and concluded that only eight were related to drugs (U.S. Department of Justice, National Institute of Justice, Office of Justice Programs 1993a). The striking discrep-ancy is as plausibly attributable to differences in research methods and per-sonal judgments as to any systematic differences between violence in New York and Chicago.

Spending on Illicit Drugs. Expenditures on illicit drugs provide one measure for the damage drugs do to society through crime. A consider-able share of spending on drugs is financed by property crime, and all such spending supports dealers and traffickers and the violent crime that accompanies their activities. Total expenditures on illicit drugs in 2000 are estimated to be just over $60 billion, roughly 1 percent of personal consumption expenditures, down from $134 billion (in constant dollars) in 1988 (U.S. Office of National Drug Control Policy 2001a). With the possible exception of alcohol during prohibition, it is likely that no other illicit market has ever generated such a large income to sellers, expressed as a percentage of gross domestic product (GDP). Most drug money goes to those at the bottom of the distribution system, who earn modest incomes; in Washington, D.C., it was estimated that in 1988 the average street dealer working four or five days a week earned about $25,000 a year (Reuter, MacCoun, and Murphy 1990).

The earnings figure has almost certainly dropped since the late 1980s, as the markets have matured and the user population has become more marginalized. Bourgois (1996) describes the desperate lives of impoverished crack sellers in East Harlem, where monetary earnings may well be less than the minimum wage, and seller-users are trapped by dysfunctional behaviors that prevent their maintaining conventional jobs.

Morbidity and Mortality. The health consequences of illicit drugs are also severe. Needle-sharing can transmit disease, and intoxication and the obsessive search for the money to purchase drugs lead to neglect of basic health among frequent users of cocaine and heroin. The Centers for Disease Control (CDC) estimates that at least 140,000 of the approximately 500,000 individuals who have died of AIDS in the United States contracted the disease from injection-drug use (U.S. Department of Health and Human Services, Centers for Disease Control and Prevention 2003a). And that does not include those who contracted AIDS from sexual contact with HIV-infected drug users. In some areas of the country, particularly in New York City with its large population of heroin addicts, the HIV rate among injection-drug users (IDUs) exceeded 50 percent at the peak of the epidemic (Des Jarlais et al. 1994). The rate has since declined, in part because so many HIV-infected IDUs have died (Des Jarlais et al. 1998). Hepatitis B and C are both rampant among IDUs.[18] IDU populations typically show Hepatitis C prevalence rates of 60–80 percent, and some samples have revealed rates as high as 95 percent (Des Jarlais and Schuchat 2001; Pollack 2001a).

The CDC's National Vital Statistics System reported 21,683 drug-induced deaths from legal and illegal drug use in 2001 (U.S. Department of Health and Human Services, Centers for Disease Control and Prevention 2003b), representing a rate of perhaps one-half of 1 percent a year of the population of frequent users of cocaine and heroin. But this figure includes only acute drug fatalities; deaths attributable to the chronic effects of drug abuse are not counted. Cohort studies of addicts (see, for example, Hser et al. 2001) find rates of mortality from all sources closer to 1 to 2 percent a year, about ten times higher than for nonaddicts of similar ages and education levels. The official number for drug-related deaths is thus likely to be a substantial underestimate of the actual total.[19]

Many health consequences of drug abuse are not side effects of the drugs themselves, but result instead from hazardous lifestyles and drug-use practices. This is not to say that drugs are safe. Acute reactions to stimulants such as PCP, cocaine, and methamphetamines are not rare; large doses of heroin can cause death from depression of the respiratory or central nervous systems; marijuana cigarettes contain more tar than tobacco cigarettes; and all psychoactive drugs can adversely affect cognitive development. But the pharmacological effects of drugs do not cause HIV/AIDS, hepatitis, and tuberculosis. Needle-sharing, unprotected sex, and other unhealthy practices are responsible for the high rates of these diseases among heavy drug users. The extent to which these practices are a function of tough enforcement in the United States is hard to tell; European addicts do not generally seem to be in much better condition, notwithstanding less aggressive enforcement. In a recent study that followed cohorts of problem drug users in nine European sites, annual mortality rates in all but two ranged between 0.9 percent and 2.3 percent (European Monitoring Centre for Drugs and Drug Addiction 2002, figure 19).[20] This is all the more striking because HIV rates have been lower among European problem drug users, compared to their American counterparts.

Homelessness, Poverty, and Parenting. Drug abuse not only increases crime; it also contributes to other social problems. It is very hard to estimate the marginal effects of drug abuse on problems such as homelessness, child abuse, poverty, and unemployment, but the high relative prevalence of drug abuse among populations with these problems cannot be fully explained by the fact that disadvantage makes drug abuse more likely.

Most studies suggest that at least one-third of the homeless have substance-abuse problems, including both drugs and alcohol (Jencks 1994). Estimates of drug abuse among welfare recipients vary widely (Pollack et al. 2002). The sounder estimates suggest that in the mid-1990s, dependence on illicit drugs was several times more common among welfare recipients than among the general population, but the rates were surprisingly low, probably less than 10 percent. The U.S. General Accounting Office (1997) has estimated that the majority of foster-care cases involve parental drug or alcohol abuse. Other research indicates that, even after controlling for social, demographic, and psychiatric variables, substance abusers are over three times as likely as others to subject their children to physical abuse (Chaffin, Kelleher, and Hollenberg 1996).

The issue of cocaine and crack use by pregnant women has received particular attention, much of it driven by predictions in the 1980s that perinatal crack use would lead to a massive cohort of brain-damaged children. Public responses to these forecasts created additional publicity, most visibly in Charleston, South Carolina, where pregnant women who sought obstetrical care at the Medical University of South Carolina were screened for cocaine use, and some who tested positive were prosecuted for child abuse. A resulting lawsuit reached the U.S. Supreme Court, which ruled in 2001 that in these circumstances a nonconsensual drug test of a patient constituted an unconstitutional search (Satel 2001).

Initial predictions of the developmental problems caused by perinatal crack use have proved overblown. That does not mean, however, that there is no "crack baby" problem. Harold Pollack (2000) has noted that "perinatal crack use is largely a pediatric problem that has been misdiagnosed as an obstetric one. Most pregnant women with serious drug problems will deliver healthy babies. However, many cannot properly care for these infants when they take them home." Crack babies are born at risk for various medical problems, but good care can do much to improve the outlook for these children. While it is desirable and useful to fund programs that reduce the risk of perinatal cocaine exposure, programs aimed at improving postpartum maternal care may be comparably, if not more, cost effective.

Productivity Losses. Drug abuse can impair productivity. It can interfere with a person's ability or willingness to develop skills and experience, find and obtain a job, and work effectively. But evidence that drug use lowers productivity is surprisingly weak. Several studies, in fact, have found that drug use is associated with higher earnings (Kaestner 1991; Register and Williams 1992). The explanation for this apparent paradox may be that in some cohorts, moderate drug use is normative behavior, and abstinence, certainly on a lifetime basis, signals a deviance for which statistical controls are hard to find. What the research suggests is that any substantial negative effects of drug use on productivity are highly concentrated, involving only a minority of users.

Drug selling may do more to reduce economic productivity than drug use. The drug trade diverts inner-city youths from legitimate pursuits of school and employment, the effects of which are compounded by high rates of arrest and incarceration that further reduce earning potential. And in many urban minority areas, the scale of this diversion is staggering. One study found that for Washington, D.C., nearly one-third of African-American males born in the 1960s were charged with drug selling between the ages of eighteen and twenty-four (Saner, MacCoun, and Reuter 1995).

Communities. "Drug use affects all Americans," the National Drug Control Strategy has emphasized (U.S. Office of National Drug Control Policy 2001b, 9). The suggestion that we're all in the same boat may be useful for the purposes of generating political support for current policies, but it conceals the reality that the social and economic distribution of drug abuse and its consequences is highly skewed. Casual marijuana use is widely distributed across income groups, but frequent use of harder drugs, along with the worst consequences of drug abuse, are highly concentrated in poor communities, especially poor urban neighborhoods.

For example, studies that assess cocaine use among pregnant women, newborns, emergency-room patients, the homeless, and criminal populations all point to much higher rates in poor urban communities (Vega et al. 1993). After a thorough review of such studies, William Brownsberger concluded that "on balance, the evidence strongly indicates that frequent cocaine use is far more prevalent in urban poverty areas than in non-urban or non-poverty areas—perhaps more than 10 times more prevalent" (1997, 359). Moreover, the effects on community development resulting from the crime and disorder of drug markets are substantial for inner cities and quite slight for the rest of the nation.

Aggregate Cost Estimates. Several studies have attempted to estimate the total economic cost of drug abuse. So far they have served primarily as rhetorical devices for the advancement of agency or advocacy group interests. In principle, though, there are several benefits of such research. Having a dollar estimate of the aggregate damage imposed on society by drug abuse helps citizens and public officials to weigh the seriousness of drug abuse against other problems that public policy aims to alleviate. Cost estimates also facilitate the evaluation of drug policy in cost-benefit terms, and, by estimating the relative costs of health care expenditures, crime, premature deaths, and so forth, can help drug policymakers set priorities.

In practice, the studies are less useful than one would hope. This does not reflect methodological weaknesses in the research as much as it does the limitations of the available data and the difficulty of the estimation task. For some components, such as driving fatalities and injuries, the researchers have lacked good data, so they have simply set the value at zero, the one number that is certain to be incorrect. For others, such as the percentage of crime attributable to drug abuse and what that crime costs society, they have made educated guesses, which is all one can do (Reuter 1999).

But educated guesses are better than no guesses, and so it is worth looking at the estimates. The most recent substantial effort to assess the total economic cost of drug abuse, sponsored by the U.S. Office of National Drug Control Policy (2001c), estimated the costs for 1992–98 and projected them through the year 2000. Table 2-3 summarizes the projected costs for 2000.

Table 2-3 presents a number of problems. For one thing, these estimates attempt to include all of the budgetary costs of drug policy, although that is not clear from the labels used. Federal funds spent on supply reduction, for example, are included in the category of "Cost of Goods and Services Lost to Crime," as are police, judicial, and correction costs attributable to drug abuse. However, beyond the identification of budgetary items, the estimates do not distinguish between costs that are attributable to drug abuse and those that represent side effects of drug policy. In theory, such an accounting would be useful, but it does not appear feasible. Estimating the percentage of, say, burglaries attributable to drug abuse is difficult enough; estimating the share of burglaries that should be blamed on drug policy as opposed to drug abuse would be an exercise in conjecture.[21]

It should be noted that the bottom line in table 2-3—$161 billion in total economic costs attributable to drug abuse—is close to the high end of the range for other similar studies, adjusting for inflation and population growth, and is probably close to the costs attributable to alcohol abuse.[22] It is also worth noting that lacking in these figures is any estimate of the difference between costs associated with the "average" and "marginal" user—that is, the user who is likely to drop out under a particular policy intervention. Suppose that another $1 billion in treatment expenditures were to reduce cocaine consumption by 2 percent; would that reduce the total costs of cocaine abuse by more or less than 2 percent? It might be that the marginal drug users treated would be the most harmful of those currently dependent, so that the marginal

TABLE 2-3

ECONOMIC COSTS OF DRUG ABUSE IN THE UNITED STATES, 2000

(millions of dollars)

Cost Categories	Estimated Cost
Health Care	
Community-Based Drug-Abuse Treatment	$5,594
Federally Provided Drug-Abuse Treatment	$506
Support for Drug Abuse–Related Health Services	$2,084
Medical Consequences of Drug Abuse	$6,715
Total Health Care	$14,899
Productivity Losses	
Premature Death	$18,256
Drug Abuse–Related Illness	$25,435
Institutionalization/Hospitalization	$1,915
Productivity Loss of Victims of Crime	$2,217
Incarceration	$35,601
Crime Careers	$27,066
Total Productivity Losses	$110,491
Other Costs	
Cost of Goods and Services Lost to Crime	$35,056
Social Welfare Administration	$218
Total Other Costs	$35,274
Total Economic Costs	**$160,664**

SOURCE: U.S. Office of National Drug Control Policy 2001c.

effect was greater than 2 percent. Alternatively, those who entered treatment might be the least problematic of those currently dependent, in which case the 2 percent reduction in use would be associated with less than a 2 percent drop in cocaine-related costs. In addition, these estimates are aggregated across all drugs and do not readily break down into drug-specific components.

Our purpose in presenting these figures is not to endorse or criticize them. In our view, what is most useful in these cost estimates is the relative size of the different cost components. In particular, the various direct and indirect effects of crime comprise 62 percent of the total costs. Crime and criminal justice are the central elements of the costs of illicit drugs in contemporary American society, so reducing them must be an important goal of drug policy.

3

Current Policies

Overview

Drug-control programs are generally classified as either prevention, treatment, or enforcement, though these categories can readily be subdivided. This chapter provides a description of how these programs operate, while the next chapter assesses what is known about how well each works.

We begin with the federal drug control budget, which is the object of much of the political struggling over drug policy. Public concern about drugs and crime has been reflected in the expansion of federal spending. And arguments about appropriate policies, particularly in the early 1990s, have been captured in debates about the allocation of the budget between supply-side programs (domestic enforcement, interdiction, and international programs) and demand-side programs (treatment and prevention). However, as we will show, the federal drug control budget is not really a budget or indeed much of a reflection of the substance of the nation's drug policy. Among other things, the federal budget is misleading because it ignores the comparably large expenditures by state and local governments on the same general programs.

There is also a major complication in looking at the federal budget. In 2003, the Office of National Drug Control Policy developed a new budget concept that led to much lower estimates of total expenditures. According to ONDCP,

> Rather than being based on estimates derived after decisions were made, as was the case in previous years, with few exceptions this budget reflects actual dollars identified in the congressional

presentations of drug control agencies that accompany the annual submission of the President's budget. Additionally, the budget reflects only those expenditures aimed at reducing drug use rather than, as in the past, those associated with the consequences of drug use. (The latter are reported periodically in *The Economic Costs of Drug Abuse in the United States.*) (U.S. Office of National Drug Control Policy 2003, 6)

We continue to use the old figures for two reasons, one pragmatic and the other of principle. The pragmatic justification is that the new series has only been estimated for the period 1988 onward. The issue of principle is that ONDCP's new approach excludes from the budget some major items, such as incarceration of federal drug prisoners. In the new framework, incarceration is regarded as essentially passive, a consequence of drug use. In fact, incarceration at the federal level, which accounted for $2.4 billion in spending in fiscal year 2003, represents a major drug-control expenditure; arrest without incarceration would be much less of a deterrent and have no incapacitative effect. The expenditure is not one easily controlled by policymakers, as discussed below. While recognizing the justification for the new budget figures for a policy agency, we believe that the old ones better represent the costs of drug control. The change not only reduces total expenditures; it also substantially lowers the share accounted for by enforcement programs, from about 65 percent to 55 percent.

The Dynamics of the Drug-Control Budget

The Growth of the Federal Budget. Figure 3-1 shows the federal drug-control budget, adjusted for inflation, for the period 1985–2001, along with its breakdown among international programs, interdiction, domestic enforcement, prevention, and treatment. As illustrated, the inflation-adjusted total grew from approximately $4 billion in 1985 to about $18 billion in 2001.

Growth in the drug-control budget was always faster than in the federal budget generally, but it was particularly rapid in the period 1985–92,

FIGURE 3-1

FEDERAL DRUG CONTROL SPENDING BY FUNCTION, 1985–2001

(billions of 2001 dollars)

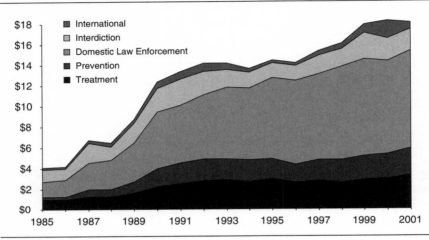

SOURCE: U.S. Office of National Drug Control Policy 1997, 2002b.

when concern about illegal drugs was at its height; the total budget grew fourfold in that seven-year period.

As the drug problem appeared to worsen during the late 1980s, rising to the top of the list of national problems in opinion polls in 1989, Congress sought to increase spending to demonstrate its own concern about the issue. Agencies were motivated to label a high share of their budgets as drug-related, since doing so made their appropriation requests more acceptable politically. The Secret Service even tried to sneak in the cost of protecting Betty Ford, who had a strong interest in the promotion of substance abuse programs; the budget examiners at ONDCP laughed that one off, but it was symptomatic of the games agencies played at that time.

Four aspects of the drug-control budget history deserve mention. First, enforcement programs have dominated throughout. The share devoted to domestic enforcement and international programs (primarily aimed at reducing supply to the United States) has fluctuated only modestly between 65 and 69 percent since 1985. Indeed, it is striking that the Clinton administration, despite a substantial softening of rhetoric, failed to increase perceptibly the share going to treatment and prevention.

Second, international programs (efforts to suppress production and transshipment within source countries) have always accounted for a very small share of the total—never more than 5 percent, and more typically only 3 percent. Despite rhetorical enthusiasm, Congress has been unable to identify plausible candidates for funding overseas programs. Third, the share going to interdiction (attempts to seize drugs or couriers on their way into the United States) has fluctuated more substantially than any other major element. In 1987 it accounted for 28 percent of the total federal budget; by the mid-1990s that figure had fallen to about 10 percent, and it has risen only modestly since then. Finally, treatment expenditures have always been substantially larger than those for prevention.

The Accuracy of the Federal Drug-Control Budget. The drug budget is a peculiar budget. It is not an appropriated budget like that of, say, the Department of Labor, determined by the administration and Congress. Instead, it is a complex, after-the-fact calculation of how much money agencies claim to be spending on drug control. The numbers are highly questionable; it is likely that the federal government is spending a good deal less than it claims, particularly on treatment (Murphy et al. 2000). Moreover, there is no mechanism for shifting funds from one class of programs to another. For example, the House Appropriations Subcommittee on Labor and Health and Human Services makes decisions about expenditures within the Department of Health and Human Services; it has no authority to make transfers to programs in the Coast Guard (handled by the Subcommittee on Commerce) or even to the Department of Veterans Affairs (handled by the Subcommittee on Veterans Affairs and Housing and Urban Development).[1]

Of the $18 billion in the (old definition) federal drug budget estimated by ONDCP for 2001, only about $3–4 billion was appropriated explicitly for drug control; the appropriations for the Drug Enforcement Administration and National Institute on Drug Abuse were the principal items of that kind. For such agencies, whose activities exclusively involve drugs, Congress can clearly decide expenditure levels in light of its views about the drug problem and the appropriate roles of the agencies.

The remaining $14–15 billion was mostly hidden in agency budgets. There were a few exceptions, notably the Bureau of Prisons, which estimated its contribution to drug control straightforwardly based on the number of inmates incarcerated for drug convictions. Some agencies simply assign a fixed proportion of their total budgets to drug control. Thus the Immigration and Naturalization Service (INS) used to assign 15 percent of its budget to drug-control activities; the only way Congress could cut the INS drug-control budget by $10 million was to cut the total agency budget by $66 million. Whether 15 percent was the correct figure mattered to no one, and the INS had little incentive to get the figure right, since it did not directly affect the agency's appropriation.

Other budget estimates have relied on highly complex algorithms. For example, the Department of Veterans Affairs (VA) has estimated how many of its patients were likely to have primary drug problems, how many would have drug and alcohol problems or drug problems and other mental disorders, and so on, and then used arbitrary (though possibly reasonable) rules to estimate what proportion of its expenditures on those clients would be classified as drug treatment. Congress, when it makes decisions about the VA budget, has no idea what effect those decisions will have on the drug budget. Indeed, the VA itself has only a rough idea of what it will spend out of the forthcoming year's appropriation on drug treatment. It is scarcely surprising that the fiscal year 1991 figure for the VA in the drug budget, for example, which was $368 million when appropriated, had risen to $611 million when recalculated in fiscal year 1993 (Murphy 1994, 4). Nor is this a minor matter, since the VA has accounted for about one-third of estimated total federal treatment expenditures in recent years.

Serious problems also occur in the categorization of programmatic expenditures, as the labels of treatment and prevention are not explicitly defined for the budgetary exercise. The federal government labels as drug prevention some funds that clearly have many other purposes as well. For example, the Clinton administration's 1998 drug budget listed $620 million in requested prevention expenditures for the Department of Education's Safe and Drug-Free Schools and Communities (SDFSC) program, whose activities were clearly only loosely related to drug prevention. "For purposes of scoring the [Education] Department's drug control funds," explained ONDCP's budget summary, "the Department estimates that all funds used under this program for violence prevention also have a direct impact on drug prevention. Therefore, this drug control budget includes 100 percent of the resources for the SDFSC program" (U.S. Office of National Drug Control Policy 1997). Even more questionable was the decision to include as prevention funds $284 million from the "Crime Control Fund," money being requested for additional police, primarily in community-oriented policing roles.[2] An administration that claimed to be shifting priorities away from enforcement at a time of budget stringency was probably using creative accounting to accomplish that goal.

Totals for treatment funding are similarly questionable. For instance, the Department of Education claimed that $90 million of its vocational rehabilitation state grants for fiscal year 1998 constituted drug treatment, since some vocational rehabilitation clients are "individuals whose drug-related disabling conditions result in an impediment to education or employment" (U.S. Office of National Drug Control Policy 1997). At a minimum, that represents an expansive definition of drug treatment. Indeed, by that rationale, all social service expenditures on those who are harmed by their own drug abuse could be categorized as drug treatment.

The numbers are thus deeply flawed. They are the result of institutional biases, detached from any true budgeting process and from the genuine complexity of measuring drug-control efforts in multifunction programs. Though the examples of bias presented here have been primarily from demand-side programs, it is quite possible that the overstatement of expenditures—there is little likelihood of underestimates—is comparable on the supply side.

All this complexity confounds the attainment of programmatic balance in the federal budget. Occasional budget restrictions, intended to produce discipline in both Congress and the White House, make it hard to move money between widely disparate agencies. It is therefore essentially impossible, for example, to take out of the Coast Guard budget what it spends on drug interdiction and allocate it for treatment or prevention. If Congress wants to expand treatment and prevention it will have to appropriate more money for these, probably by taking it away from other health and education programs, since each appropriations subcommittee has a narrow jurisdiction and cannot move moneys among agencies outside of its jurisdiction. That battle is not one relished by treatment and prevention advocates; but the legerdemain of such devices as calling community-policing expenditures "prevention" is a poor substitute.

Limitations of the Federal Budget as a Policy Tool. The budget is also a poor tool for making policy decisions. To pick an easy example, the primary determinant of federal prison expenditures, as ONDCP has noted in explaining its new budgetary approach, is the law providing high mandatory minimum sentences for drug offenders in federal court, along with the guidelines established by the United States Sentencing Commission.[3] If Congress wishes to spend less on incarcerating drug offenders, it will have to cut those minimal levels and/or direct the Department of Justice to curtail its investigation or prosecution of drug offenders. Reducing the prison budget will only mean that those who are sentenced will either have to be released earlier or spend their sentences in more crowded and ill-serviced facilities. While the first option is almost certainly a sensible one at the federal level, it is not easily implemented without a parole board, which was abolished by Congress in the Sentencing Reform Act of 1984.

A focus on budgets also tends to obscure important differences among programs. The broadest labels, supply-side and demand-side, are admittedly crude ones, but the slightly more refined categorization of enforcement, treatment, and prevention is also basically flawed. William Bennett, in his eloquent introduction to the first National Drug Control Strategy, objected to the demand side/supply side split, arguing that enforcement could directly reduce demand (U.S. Office of National Drug Control Policy 1989, 12–13). After all, effective enforcement should raise the price and reduce the availability of illicit drugs, thereby decreasing consumption.[4]

It is true that enforcement against drug retailers can reduce demand. Mark Moore noted in 1973 that only street-level enforcement can, in theory, raise the nonmonetary costs of purchasing drugs, by making them riskier or harder to find, thus lowering demand. However, since the federal government attempts to confine itself to higher-level enforcement rather than street-level transactions—convictions for possession offenses have constituted only about 15 percent of total federal drug convictions in recent years—the usual categorization of supply and demand programs is correct for the federal budget, except perhaps for pass-throughs to local governments for policing. In addition, Caulkins (1998) estimated that, given what is known about the hourly earnings of addicts and the amount of time they spend searching for drugs, any increase in purchasing inconvenience resulting from enforcement is likely to have quite small effects on consumption.[5]

Enforcement strategies aimed at users, such as "sell-and-bust" tactics used in street markets, may be categorized as demand-side, albeit not of the kind that liberal advocates of treatment are likely to enthuse about.[6] Yet such enforcement may indeed constitute an effective prevention program; lack of easy access to highly visible markets may do as much to deter those adolescent experimenters who are at moderate risk of becoming regular users as any existing secondary prevention program. However, it is impossible to split out user-oriented enforcement from other kinds of local drug enforcement in budgetary terms.

A discussion of priorities then must go to the content of programs. Expanding efforts at enforced abstinence for probationers, parolees, and those out on pretrial release programs, as Mark Kleiman (1997) advocates, will appear in enforcement budgets but constitute substantially a demand-side program. Its goal is precisely to reduce the demand for drugs, but it uses the threat of penalties, aimed at those users whose behavior causes the greatest harm, to accomplish that goal.

Moreover, there are more dimensions to policy than the current budget divisions suggest. Treatment for criminal justice referrals has very different consequences for drug-related harms than does treatment for pregnant women.[7] The gains from the former consist largely of reductions in crime, while the gains from the latter mostly take the form of improved health and parenting for the children of drug-involved mothers. Comparing those gains is complicated, but treatment of pregnant women is likely to appear more congruent with the "public health" approach that has become a popular slogan for drug policy reformers than is treatment of high-rate criminal offenders.[8] However, if one takes the broad view of public health, in which violence is seen as a major cause of injury to health, then the latter might be the preferred program.

Theoretically, drug policy might best be categorized not by characteristics of program instruments (enforcement, treatment, prevention) but by the nature of the harms reduced (crime, accidents, illness, and so on). Unfortunately, that is neither empirically nor politically feasible. Nonetheless, the realization that different programs confer very different kinds of benefits, and that their principal beneficiaries also vary greatly, helps point up the weakness of the current classification system.

State and Local Expenditures. The focus on the federal budget is particularly inappropriate because lower levels of government spend significant amounts of money out of their own funds on drug control. If budgets matter, then it is important to develop estimates of these non-federal expenditures and of mechanisms that might lead to a change in their composition.

Unfortunately, the only available estimates of state and local spending are quite old. ONDCP commissioned the Census Bureau to conduct a detailed study of state and local expenditures on drug control in 1990 and 1991 (U.S. Bureau of the Census 1993). The Census estimate was admittedly incomplete because it did not include expenditures by specialized units of government, such as independent school districts and special districts (including independent hospital authorities).[9] Nevertheless, the study came up with a total of $14.1 billion for 1990 and $15.9 billion for 1991. When one subtracts out the estimated $3.2 billion in federal transfer payments to the state and local governments in 1991, this produces a total of $12.7 billion, compared to the $11 billion spent by the federal government that year.[10]

The Census estimates for 1991 showed the state and local expenditures to be even more enforcement-oriented than those of the federal government. Though no more recent estimate is available, it is very likely that this continues to be true. First, the number of individuals entering state prison for drug convictions continued to rise into the late 1990s, even though the number of arrests had stabilized a few years earlier; moreover, inmates are serving longer sentences. Second, annual data on treatment expenditures still show that state and local governments provide a modest share of the total. Third, although prevention expenditures are the most difficult to track, since there is no centralized appropriation for drug prevention in school budgets, where much of the spending occurs, there is no indication of a substantial increase.

The continued rapid rise in commitments to state prison for drug offenses suggests that state and local expenditures have roughly kept pace with the growth in federal spending. Ignoring state and local budgets distorts perceptions of policy within the United States. If these budgets are included, then the share of drug-control expenditures going to treatment and prevention probably falls from one-third to about one-quarter. And the share going to interdiction becomes around 5 percent, rather than the 10 percent usually cited. If budgets are to be truly useful for drug-policy-making purposes, the overlap between the domestic federal programs and those of state and local governments makes it essential to create a true national budget.

We now turn to examining the content of the activities under the major programmatic categories.

Enforcement

Cocaine and heroin are distributed down a long chain, from overseas production to sale on the street or in the dormitory. Each link in the distribution chain presents a different set of enforcement opportunities and is associated with its own agencies and institutions. For example, suppressing production and export in other countries is primarily a responsibility of the State Department and the Department of Defense. At the other end of the distribution system, street enforcement is principally carried out by local police departments, with state courts and prisons disposing of the arrests. Rather than treat it as a single set of programs, then, we break the enforcement system into four components: source-country control, interdiction, high-level domestic enforcement, and street-level enforcement. For each we briefly describe current policies and how they affect drug problems.

Source-Country Control. Since most illicit drugs consumed in the United States are produced abroad, many have concluded that programs aimed at reducing production or export from the source countries can make a difference to U.S. drug problems. International programs therefore attract a great deal of political attention. The intersection of overseas drug cultivation and trafficking with other foreign policy concerns has made these programs even more prominent, particularly in Colombia, where the guerillas challenging the central government are financially dependent on coca growing, and Afghanistan, where opium production has returned to world-leading levels despite a ban enacted by President Hamid Karzai.

The sources of supply to the United States have never been very diverse. In the early 1990s, Bolivia, Peru, and Colombia were the predominant sources of cocaine, while most heroin was imported from Afghanistan, Burma (now Myanmar), and Mexico. Since 1995, overseas sources have become even more concentrated. Colombia now dominates the production, refining, and export of cocaine, with Bolivia and Peru of secondary importance in the growing of coca. Colombia has also supplanted Asian sources in the U.S. heroin market (U.S. Department of Justice, Drug Enforcement Administration 2002). Mexico and Colombia now account for about two-thirds of U.S. heroin imports, even though Afghanistan and Myanmar have accounted for about 90 percent of world opium production in most recent years (United Nations Office for Drug Control and Crime Prevention 2002). Mexico is the principal source of imported marijuana and methamphetamine, though a substantial share of both of these drugs is produced domestically.

Three types of programs have been tried to reduce source-country drug production: eradication, alternative crop development, and in-country enforcement. Eradication, usually involving aerial spraying but sometimes ground-based operations, aims either to literally limit the quantity of the drugs available for shipment to the United States, to raise the cost of producing those drugs, or to otherwise discourage farmers from growing them. Alternative development is the soft version of this; it encourages farmers growing coca or poppies to switch to legitimate crops by increasing earnings from these other products. Strategies include introducing new crops and more productive strains of traditional crops, improving transportation for getting the crops to market, and implementing various marketing and subsidy schemes. Finally, the United States pushes source countries to pursue traffickers and refiners more vigorously, often providing military equipment and training.

None of these programs receives much money. In fiscal year 2002, even with the much-trumpeted Plan Colombia, expenditures overseas totaled only $1.1 billion out of a total federal drug-control budget of $18.8 billion (old definition). The vast majority of that money went to the

Andean region, since Mexico has so far, as a matter of national sovereignty, been unwilling to allow the operation of U.S. programs on its territory. And although Asia is the dominant region for heroin production, there have been no meaningful opportunities to intervene in the major producing nations there, Afghanistan and Myanmar, as the United States did not have an ambassador in either country for over a decade. The 2001 war against the Taliban may eventually produce opportunities for reducing opium production, as the new government works toward control in growing regions and seeks Western approval and economic assistance.[11] But after a steep decline in 2001, opium production in Afghanistan surged in 2002, accounting, according to United Nations estimates, for nearly three-quarters of global output (United Nations Office on Drugs and Crime 2003b). As of November 2004, the United Nations Office on Drugs and Crime estimates that Afghan production is near record levels.

Few countries are willing to allow aerial eradication. It can cause environmental damage and is also politically unattractive, since the immediate targets, peasant farmers, are among the poorest citizens, even when growing coca or poppy. Colombia and Mexico, neither a traditional producer of drugs, have been the source countries most willing to allow spraying. For these governments the campaign has not involved an attack on indigenous ways, though often on indigenous peoples.

Aerial eradication has had one significant, if short-lived, success story: the drop in Mexican opium production in the mid-1970s. An industry that had operated fairly openly in five northern states, with large, unprotected fields, took approximately five years to adjust to spraying. Production subsequently became much more widely dispersed, and growing fields were reduced in size and hidden in remote locations. By the early 1980s, Mexico was supplying as much heroin as before the spraying, but for about five years there was a substantial reduction in availability in the United States, particularly in western regions where Mexican supply dominated heroin markets.

Alternative development presents a very different challenge to source-country governments. In contrast to spraying, it is politically attractive, since it involves government increasing services to marginalized farmers. However, unless farmers believe the government will maintain its commitment over a long period, they will not be willing to incur the costs of shifting crops. In situations of political instability there will understand-ably be skepticism about the ability of, say, the Bolivian government to assure a dependable market and a reliable transportation infrastructure for pineapples from the Chapare. Though there are a few instances of well-executed local crop-substitution programs, it does not appear that they have reduced drug production in any region of the world.

The United States has also invested in building institutional capacity to deal with the drug trade. Each year the State Department, in its annual *International Narcotics Control Strategy Report* (*INCSR*), argues that the cen-tral problem of drug control in other countries is a lack of political will and integrity (see, for example, U.S. Department of State 2003, II-10). Training investigators, strengthening the judiciary, and improving extradition proce-dures are the stuff of efforts to deal with this issue. Unfortunately, in both Colombia and Mexico, the corruption problems have been seemingly end-less, embedded in a larger system of weak integrity controls. For example, in Colombia, where the army has taken on a major role in drug control, particularly with respect to coca growing, allegations of military involve-ment in mass killings are well substantiated and have been a major source of controversy about U.S. funding.

Since 1986, the president of the United States has been required to certify that each major producer and transshipment nation has cooper-ated fully in trying to reduce production and trafficking.[12] If a nation is not certified, the United States will withhold certain aid and trade prefer-ences and vote against loans in multilateral finance institutions, such as the Asian Development Bank. Whatever the rationale for this process, it has been tarnished in practice by its obvious divorce from drug control. Certain pariah nations, such as Nigeria (until recently) and Myanmar, are always decertified, while the largest single source for the United States market, Mexico, with its long history of corruption in drug-control efforts, is always granted certification.[13] The political costs of decertifying Mexico, given the close and complex relations between Mexico and the United States, are unacceptably high. The one strategic use of decertification occurred in 1995–96, when the Clinton administration decertified the Samper government in Colombia, following allegations that drug traffickers had financed Samper's presidential campaign. This turned out to have little effect on collaboration between agencies in the two countries; it simply meant that the president's office in Colombia became isolated from the rest of the government.

At present, with an increasing acceptance that the U.S. drug problem is less attributable to other nations' production than to domestic demand, support may be growing for a repeal of the certification law. Certification, if it remains, will continue to be no more than ritualistic, though the annual report required by the law is often helpful on problems of drug control in each nation. The 2001 statement by President George W. Bush, at a meeting with Mexican president Vicente Fox, that the fundamental problem is Americans' demand for these drugs, has, as noted in chapter 1, helped take the energy out of the certification process.

Interdiction. A surprising number of Americans believe that the federal government must be complicit in the drug trade, because otherwise such vast quantities of drugs would not be able to enter the country. But these quantities, though generating tens of billions of dollars in sales ($35 billion for cocaine; $10 billion for heroin, according to ONDCP estimates), are in fact tiny volumes. Including what is seized at the borders and in the interior, imports are estimated at about fifteen tons for heroin and four hundred tons for cocaine.

Given the enormous volume of traffic and commerce across U.S. borders, particularly from Mexico and the Caribbean, it is not hard to hide a few hundred tons. Indeed, it can be seen as remarkable that interdiction seizes such a large share of cocaine production—perhaps 35–40 percent over the whole production, international transport, and domestic distribution system. Heroin seizures come closer to the 10 percent that orthodoxy has enshrined as the share generally seized by enforcement agencies, but this is because most heroin enters the country in small packages, reducing the potential for seizure.[14]

Interdiction was the principal federal enforcement program in the mid-1980s, when there was an outcry in Congress for the Department of Defense (DoD) to "seal the borders." DoD was asked to take on a major role, augmenting the efforts of the Coast Guard and Customs Service. In practice, DoD provides some actual interdiction resources but is mostly involved in coordination and intelligence. Since the early 1990s interdiction has attracted little political attention beyond the occasional call for increases. Interestingly, polls consistently show that at least half of the

American public believes interdiction is the most promising way of controlling drugs (Pew Research Center for the People and the Press 2001).

The quantity of cocaine seized has fluctuated between around 105 and 140 tons since the late 1980s, reflecting the flatness of estimated consumption over the same period (U.S. Office of National Drug Control Policy 2001a). There is more variation in the heroin figure; at 1–2 tons, the total can be affected by a small number of large seizures.

Interdiction involves an unending series of adaptations by both smugglers and enforcement agencies. There are large-scale shifts in routes, modes of transportation, and techniques for hiding drugs. In the early 1980s much cocaine entered the United States through Florida, but an early Reagan interdiction effort, run by then vice president George H. W. Bush, pushed traffickers farther out in the Caribbean and into Mexico. Mexico is said to remain the dominant route, but there is some evidence of renewed smuggling through the Caribbean.

In the 1980s, a large share (no more precise statement can be made) of cocaine was brought in by private planes, typically carrying 250 to 500 kilograms on each trip. By the early 1990s, smugglers had shifted to intermingling their loads with legitimate commerce, especially in trucks crossing the border between Mexico and the United States, a method of conveyance thought to have become more common following the North American Free Trade Agreement (NAFTA).

Technological innovations in detection are announced from time to time, such as machines that can scan containers from the outside and identify cocaine through its pattern of heat reflection. We have no way of determining how any of these innovations individually affects the drug trade. We can say that by official estimates, drug import prices have not risen, suggesting little increase in the effective risk of smuggling; and there seems only a modest diminution in the total volume of drugs entering the country.

High-Level Enforcement. A larger share of the federal drug budget goes to efforts to investigate, arrest, prosecute, and imprison those involved in the distribution of large quantities of drugs than to interdiction. One cannot say that such funding goes to capturing more important or larger distributors because, in fact, most of those caught have quite minor trafficking roles;

FIGURE 3-2

SENTENCED DRUG OFFENDERS IN FEDERAL PRISONS, 1970–2002

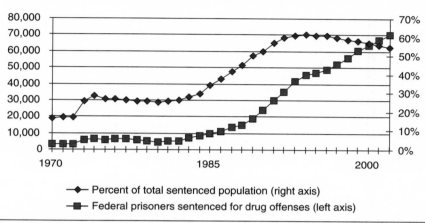

━◆━ Percent of total sentenced population (right axis)

━■━ Federal prisoners sentenced for drug offenses (left axis)

SOURCE: U.S. Department of Justice, Federal Bureau of Prisons 2003.

they are agents for senior traffickers. This reflects on the one hand that there are many more agents than principals, and on the other that the principals invest more in protecting themselves from detection.[15] An internal 1993 study by the U.S. Department of Justice estimated that more than half of those convicted in federal court were involved in retailing activities.

Drug dealers dominate the federal prison population: In 2002, federal prisons held some 70,000 inmates sentenced for drug offenses, an all-time high. The annual fiscal cost associated with this imprisonment is about $2.5 billion. Drug offenders constituted 55 percent of inmates in federal prisons in 2002, a share somewhat below the 61 percent peak "achieved" in 1994, but still a far higher fraction than for any year in the 1970s or 1980s. Figure 3-2 shows the massive increase in federal incarceration of drug offenders over the past three decades, both in absolute numbers and as a share of the total federal prison population. There has been a rise both in the length of drug-related sentences (from seventy months in 1986 to eighty-eight months in 1994, and then falling to seventy-nine months in 1999) and the share of those sentences actually served; by 1999 the fraction was about four-fifths, reflecting the combined impact of mandatory minimum sentencing statutes and the guidelines of the U.S. Sentencing Commission, as well as the end of parole in the federal system.

It should also be noted that federal drug enforcement imposes on traffickers significant nonimprisonment costs through the seizure of drugs, and the seizure and forfeiture of other assets. These costs exceed $1 billion annually, which can be thought of as a tax on the higher levels of the trade.

Sentencing policy has been the principal focus of discussion about federal drug enforcement. Particularly controversial is the discrepancy between mandatory sentences for crack and for cocaine powder—the sale of five grams of crack brings a mandatory five-year sentence, but for powder, the triggering quantity for the same sentence is 500 grams. This difference turns out to have a racially disparate impact; African-Americans are much more commonly charged federally with crack distribution than with distribution of powder. Congress has been unwilling to act on this matter, despite urging by then attorney general Janet Reno and ONDCP director Barry McCaffrey in 1998, and more recently by the U.S. Sentencing Commission. At the federal level this debate is largely symbolic, since only a few hundred individuals are convicted of crack offenses each year; crack is manufactured at very low levels of the distribution system, which federal agents and prosecutors generally eschew. Many states, however, have statutes that mirror federal law in imposing longer sentences for crack offenses than for cocaine, and here the racially disparate impacts are significant because of the much larger numbers of crack dealers sentenced in state courts.

Some have argued that relatively tougher penalties for crack offenses are the product of a deliberate targeting of minorities for punishment (Tonry 1995), but in our view racism doesn't explain the disparity in penalties. As Randall Kennedy has pointed out, the Anti-Drug Abuse Act of 1986, which established different sentences for crack and powder cocaine, passed with the support of eleven of the twenty black members of Congress, including Charles Rangel, who chaired the House Select Committee on Narcotics Abuse and Control (Kennedy 1997). In 1997, Rangel introduced legislation to remove the distinction between powder and crack cocaine in federal sentencing, but in 1986, when crack dealing and use were devastating urban minority communities, he, like most black politicians, felt that the much greater danger crack posed to those communities justified the disparity.

There are larger issues of sentencing policy. Are long sentences appropriate for drug offenses, in particular for those offenders who are only agents for high-level traffickers? And should sentences be related to the quantity of drugs involved? Some individual cases can fairly be considered horror stories, where quite minor figures have received very long sentences because they appeared in the investigations of major trafficking operations and were unwilling to provide information in return for reduced sentences (see Schlosser 1994, 1997). The sentencing guidelines structure is rigid, as it is for other offenses as well, and some federal judges have rebelled. Most notably, District Judge Jack Weinstein, exercising the prerogative of a senior judge, removed himself from hearing drug cases in the Eastern District of New York. Judge Weinstein acknowledged discomfort in shifting the "dirty work" to other judges but said, "At the moment . . . I simply cannot sentence another impoverished person whose destruction has no discernible effect on the drug trade. . . . I am just a tired old judge who has temporarily filled his quota of remorselessness" (quoted in Minow 1997).

Federal drug enforcement is particularly intrusive toward state and local enforcement. There is considerable overlap between the jurisdictions of federal and other agencies, and many cases are brought by "task forces" of federal and local agencies. Local agencies often have an incentive to cooperate with federal agencies because asset-seizure rules under federal law are more generous to them than the comparable state rules. This is not a problem in principle; improved coordination is desirable. Some observers believe, however, that intrusive federal drug enforcement has had the effect of limiting local discretion. And there is always the question of whether the revenues from asset seizures negatively affect enforcement strategy. For example, enforcement against emerging drugs, with smaller and less visible markets, will typically generate less asset-seizure revenue than enforcement against cocaine. There have also been raids aimed at users and minor sellers who have highly valued assets, a few of which have led to deaths of innocent people.

Retail Enforcement. Most people locked up for drug offenses are street-level offenders, apprehended and punished by local police and prosecutors

FIGURE 3-3

ARRESTS FOR DRUG LAW VIOLATIONS, BY DRUG, 1980–2003

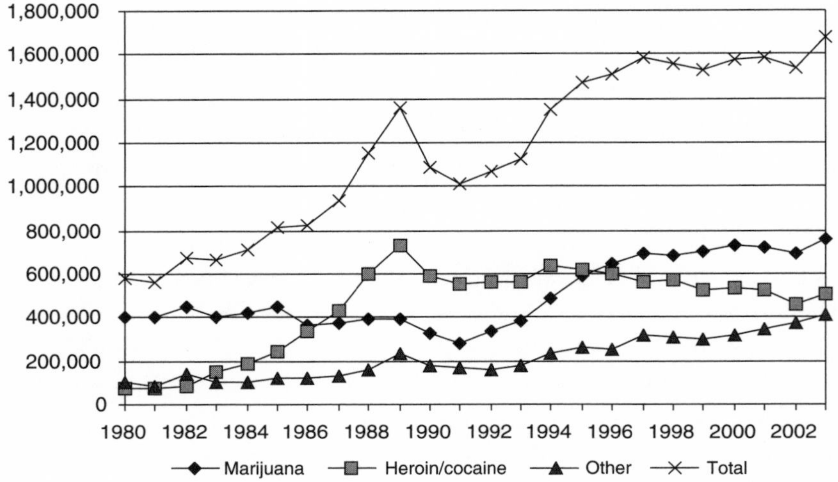

SOURCE: U.S. Department of Justice, Federal Bureau of Investigation, 1997; U.S. Department of Justice, Bureau of Justice Statistics 2004.

and imprisoned in county jails or state prisons. Punishment of drug users and sellers has increased greatly since 1981, when concern about cocaine became prominent. Arrests have more than doubled, rising from 581,000 in 1980 to nearly 1,600,000 in 2000 (from 5.5 percent to 11 percent of total arrests). But a much greater increase has occurred in the extent of imprisonment and other penalties. The number of commitments to state and federal prison, for example, has risen approximately tenfold. (Figures 3-3 and 3-4 depict changes over the past twenty years.)

The key to understanding the shift in punishment is to examine the composition of the arrests. There have been two dominating developments. First, from 1980 to 1989, arrests surged primarily as a result of a tenfold increase in heroin and cocaine arrests. In 1980, 68 percent of arrests were for marijuana, whereas heroin and cocaine accounted for 13 percent. In 1989, by contrast, 54 percent of arrests involved heroin or cocaine. Then, from 1990 to 2000, marijuana arrests more than doubled, while heroin and cocaine arrests declined slightly.

FIGURE 3-4

NUMBER OF PERSONS UNDER STATE AND FEDERAL CUSTODY FOR DRUG
OFFENSES, 1980–2001

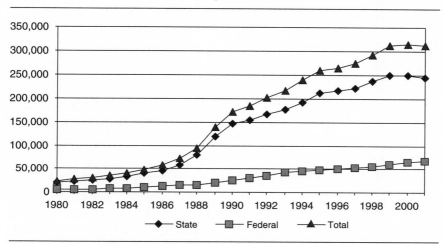

SOURCE: U.S. Department of Justice, Bureau of Justice Statistics 2003b; U.S. Department of Justice, Federal Bureau of Prisons 2003.

The reasons for the increase in marijuana arrests are difficult to discern; overall use did not increase during that period, and there was no declared crackdown policy in most jurisdictions. Blacks and adolescents were particularly affected by the rise. Black arrest rates for marijuana possession were equal to those for whites in 1992; by 2000, black rates were twice as high. The rise for adolescents was even greater, about sevenfold. Even after adjusting for increased use among adolescents, the risk of arrest for a teenage user increased by several hundred percent. Though a negligible number of arrests resulted in jail or prison terms, a study of a sample of marijuana arrestees in three Maryland counties found that almost one-third spent some time in jail prior to trial (Reuter, Hirschfield, and Davies 2001).

Conviction and imprisonment levels have increased more sharply and consistently than arrests. From 1986, the first year of consistent reporting, to 1990, felony convictions for drug trafficking in state courts more than doubled (U.S. Department of Justice, Bureau of Justice Statistics 1993). Between 1990 and 1998, the number of felony drug-trafficking convictions in state courts nearly doubled again (U.S. Department of Justice, Bureau of Justice Statistics 2001). The percentage of such convictions resulting in prison sentences also rose, though not by as much. In 1998, state courts imposed prison sentences in 45 percent of felony drug-trafficking convictions, compared to 36 percent in 1986.

Led by Congress, state legislatures have passed statutes mandating longer sentences for drug offenders. This has not apparently led to much increase in average time served at the state level, probably because low-level offenders more often receive short sentences instead of probation, offsetting the longer sentences for high-level offenders. Average sentences are now at around forty-eight months, of which about one-half is actually served.

Taken by themselves, sentencing figures are insufficient to show that enforcement has become more stringent; the degree of punitiveness depends upon the ratio of sentences (or years of prison time) to offenses. Estimating the number of offenses (or at least the rate of change in that number) is in itself a highly speculative task. We believe that the number of offenses might have risen as rapidly as arrests, sentences, and years of prison time between 1980 and 1985, but after 1985 it is very likely that the number of offenses and offenders (sales and sellers) was essentially flat, and that the stringency of enforcement became greater.

How risky is drug selling or possession? The aggregate data suggest that the 1999 risk of being arrested for marijuana possession, conditional on using marijuana in the previous year, was about 3 percent; for cocaine the figure was 6 percent. For drug-selling, a RAND study of the District of Columbia estimated that in 1988, street dealers of drugs faced about a 22 percent probability of imprisonment in the course of a year's selling and that, given the expected amount of time served, they spent about one-third of their selling careers in prison (Reuter, MacCoun, and Murphy 1990). These figures were consistent with crude calculations at the national level at that time; they have certainly grown since then.

Does this level of enforcement make drug selling appropriately risky? One-third of a career in prison seems quite a lot. On the other hand, the risk per sale is very small indeed. A seller who works two days a week at this trade may make 1,000 transactions in the course of a year. His imprisonment risk per transaction in the 1988 Washington, D.C., study just cited was only about 1 in 4,500; by that measure, each transaction was a great deal less risky than, say, a burglary or robbery. Also, the expected cell-years per dollar earned was low relative to property crimes.

Another way to consider the risk is to look at aggregate figures. American users consume an estimated three hundred tons of pure cocaine a year. If sold in 0.2-gram units, this volume would involve 1.5 billion transactions, which generate fewer than 100,000 prison sentences—or less than a 1 in 15,000 risk of imprisonment per sale. These are merely indicative figures; the correct number is probably less than 1 in 5,000 and more than 1 in 20,000.

In many ways these figures reflect the realities of committing property crimes as well. The probability of an individual robbery or burglary leading to imprisonment is slight, but robbers and burglars make it up in volume; most who commit these crimes regularly spend a substantial amount of time in prison. The difference between property and drug crimes is the volume of transactions; few burglars manage to commit a thousand felonies a year, as do many retail drug dealers.

It is hard to analyze drug enforcement in contemporary America without reference to race (Tonry 1995). Those arrested for drug selling are predominantly minorities; that disproportion is even higher for prison sentences. In 1999, blacks, who constitute 12 percent of the population, comprised 60 percent of those admitted to state prison for drug offenses, compared to slightly less than one-half for all nondrug offenses. Hispanics (about 10 percent of the general population) accounted for 25 percent of commitments for drug offenses, compared to about 15 percent for nondrug offenses. The principal explanation for these disparities is probably that retail dealing (particularly in open settings) and heavy use of cocaine and heroin are concentrated in poor minority communities.

Treatment

The range of activities comprising "drug treatment" is vast, since almost any structured effort designed to reduce use or otherwise improve drug-related behavior among the addicted can be considered drug treatment. When an inmate with a history of drug abuse attends a prison-based drug abuse counseling session, or a heroin addict receives methadone from an outpatient clinic, or a cocaine-using stockbroker seeks help from a private-practice

TABLE 3-1
COMMON DRUG TREATMENT MODALITIES

Modality	Brief Description
Methadone Maintenance	Ambulatory programs that provide methadone hydrochloride, a long-term pharmacological treatment for opiate dependence.
Therapeutic Communities (TCs)	Residential programs; typical stays are nine to twelve months.
Outpatient Nonmethadone Programs	Programs employ a variety of treatment approaches; generally provide individual or group counseling once or twice weekly for a period averaging six months.
Chemical Dependency (CD) Programs	Three- to six-week inpatient or residential programs based on a twelve-step model; used more for alcohol than drug treatment.
Detoxification	Medically supervised withdrawal to abstinence over a short period, usually five to seven days.

psychiatrist, or an overdose victim is detoxified in a hospital, or an ex–drug abuser attends a Narcotics Anonymous session in a church basement, treatment is being provided. Treatment involves various modalities, delivered to multiple population groups by different types of individuals and organizations, in a range of settings, paid for by a variety of funding sources.

There is no universally accepted approach to classifying such diverse activities. Clinicians often view treatment in terms of different therapeutic approaches: "Relapse prevention," "the matrix model," "supportive–expressive psychotherapy," and "motivational enhancement therapy" are among the common labels (U.S. Department of Health and Human Services, National Institute on Drug Abuse 1999). By contrast, private insurers are more likely to make distinctions that reflect cost differences, considering in particular whether care is provided on an inpatient or outpatient basis, and for what period of time. Policymakers usually talk of treatment "modalities," a term that in practice makes distinctions among both care settings and treatment approaches. Table 3-1 provides a typical list of modalities.

The heterogeneity of treatment activities makes it especially difficult to gather valid, or even consistent, data on the treatment system. The complex array of funding sources, providers, and activities makes treatment hard to categorize. It also makes it hard to identify and keep track of treatment activities, especially given the overlap of drug treatment with alcohol treatment and other mental health and social services.

Overview of the Treatment System. The federal government estimates that total expenditures on drug abuse treatment, including the costs of health-related services, were $5.5 billion in 1997, the most recent year for which comprehensive government estimates are available (U.S. Department of Health and Human Services, Substance Abuse and Mental Health Services Administration 2001a). This comprised about 46 percent of total spending for all substance abuse treatment. Expenditures on alcohol abuse for that year were $6.4 billion (54 percent of the total). Since many programs provide treatment both for alcohol and other drug problems and many clients abuse both alcohol and an illicit drug, data systems do not always report drug treatment figures separately.

It is estimated that private sources funded 38.5 percent of drug abuse treatment in 1997, with private insurance contributing 61 percent of that share. The federal government paid for 33 percent of drug abuse treatment, and state and local governments covered the remaining 29 percent. Medicaid was the largest component of public spending on drug abuse treatment, accounting for 32 percent of public outlays. Other major components included Medicare, the Department of Veterans Affairs, and federal block grants, which were provided to states in proportion to their shares of the estimated number of dependent drug users. As noted in the first section of this chapter, these expenditure figures were almost certainly substantial overestimates.

Client Characteristics. Although drug addiction exists in all socioeconomic groups, it is far more common in disadvantaged populations. In 2002, according to data from the Substance Abuse and Mental Health Services Administration's Treatment Episode Data Set (TEDS), only 25 percent of adult drug treatment clients (those whose primary substance of abuse was an illicit drug and not alcohol) were employed, and 37 percent did not have a high school degree or GED (U.S. Department of Health and Human Services, Substance Abuse and Mental Health

Services Administration 2004b). Although 55 percent of admitted treatment clients were white, this percentage was influenced by more substantial white majorities for marijuana and stimulants. Two-thirds of crack clients, and slightly more than half of heroin clients, were minorities. Since good data are unavailable on the racial breakdown of heavy heroin and crack users, it is hard to judge if drug-dependent minorities are less likely to receive treatment than drug-dependent whites.

Males represent 68 percent of those admitted to drug treatment facilities. The age of clients varies considerably according to drug. The average age at admission of marijuana clients is twenty-three years, and those who primarily abuse inhalants or hallucinogens are twenty-four years old on average. By contrast, the average age of crack clients is thirty-seven years, and the average age of heroin clients is thirty-six.

Heroin and other opiates are the primary drug of abuse in 33 percent of drug treatment admissions for which the drug is specified in the TEDS database; cocaine (including crack) is the primary drug of abuse in 24 percent of admissions. Since there are probably twice as many heavy cocaine users as heavy heroin users, this indicates that heroin addicts are at least twice as likely as cocaine addicts to receive treatment. Marijuana, the most widely used drug, accounts for 28 percent of treatment admissions. Stimulants are the primary drug of abuse in 12 percent of admissions. Other drugs, including tranquilizers, sedatives, hallucinogens, inhalants, and PCP, account for only 3 percent of admissions.

Curiously, although marijuana is a much smaller contributor to crime than heroin or crack, 58 percent of treatment admissions where the primary drug of abuse was marijuana were criminal justice system referrals. By comparison, only 13 percent of heroin treatment admissions and 26 percent of crack admissions were criminal justice system referrals. The likely explanation for the higher marijuana figure is the large number of young individuals who enter treatment programs as part of a plea bargain or pretrial negotiations. The unfortunate irony is that many of these individuals do not have serious drug problems; at the same time, arrestees who abuse cocaine and heroin are less likely to be referred to treatment. When arrested, cocaine and heroin abusers often have long and serious criminal histories that make them ineligible for drug courts, which are the source of a growing share of treatment referrals.

Trends in Treatment Expenditures. Between the mid-1970s and the late 1980s, private funding of substance abuse treatment grew rapidly. The combination of state regulations mandating insurance benefits for mental health and substance abuse services and the widespread establishment of employee assistance programs (EAPs) led to a widespread expansion in private coverage of substance abuse treatment. In 1976, private sources contributed only 5 percent of total expenditures on drug and alcohol abuse treatment (Schlesinger and Dorwart 1992). By 1987, private sources accounted for 48 percent of drug abuse treatment spending (and an even greater share for alcohol treatment), of which two-thirds was covered by private insurance, according to Center for Substance Abuse Treatment estimates (U.S. Department of Health and Human Services, Substance Abuse and Mental Health Services Administration 2001a).

In the late 1980s and 1990s, however, as corporations pressured health insurers to contain costs, private spending for drug treatment slowed considerably (and declined in real terms for alcohol treatment), while public funding rose sharply in the wake of increased public concern about drug abuse. By 1997, the share of drug treatment paid for by private sources had declined to an estimated 38.5 percent, as noted earlier (U.S. Department of Health and Human Services, Substance Abuse and Mental Health Services Administration 2001a). Table 3-2 illustrates this development, reporting total expenditures on drug abuse treatment, and growth rates, by type of payer, from 1987 to 1997.

Overall, growth in public expenditures on drug treatment has outpaced inflation, but it has slowed down considerably since 1992. The most notable change in table 3-2 is in the category of "other federal," of which federal block grants are the largest element. After a dramatic annual growth rate of 21.3 percent from 1987 to 1992, federal funding for drug treatment outside of public insurance programs declined slightly in real terms from 1992 to 1997. In other words, since the early 1990s, increased public funding for drug treatment has occurred entirely within the Medicaid and Medicare programs. Consistent with these expenditure figures, data from the Substance Abuse and Mental Health Administration's Uniform Facility Data Set and its predecessor—the National Drug and Alcohol Treatment Utilization Survey (NDATUS)—indicate that the number of clients in treatment increased by 54 percent from 1987 to 1992, but declined by 2 percent between 1992 and

TABLE 3-2

TOTAL ESTIMATED EXPENDITURES ON DRUG ABUSE TREATMENT, 1987–1997

Type of Payer	Expenditures (millions of dollars)			Average Annual Growth Rates, Adjusted for Inflation (%)		
	1987	1992	1997	1987–97	1987–92	1992–97
Private—Total	**1,295**	**1,682**	**2,117**	**1.9**	**1.5**	**2.4**
Out-of-Pocket	318	425	671	4.7	2.1	7.2
Private Insurance	859	1,056	1,285	1.1	0.4	1.8
Other Private	119	201	161	0.1	7.0	−6.4
Public—Total	**1,399**	**2,448**	**3,383**	**6.0**	**7.7**	**4.4**
Medicare	88	142	332	10.9	6.1	15.9
Medicaid	381	703	1,088	7.9	8.9	6.8
Other Federal	242	767	823	9.7	21.3	−0.8
Other State and Local	686	835	1,139	2.1	−3.3	4.1
Federal Total	**540**	**1,359**	**1,808**	**9.5**	**15.9**	**3.6**
State and Local Total	**859**	**1,088**	**1,575**	**3.1**	**1.0**	**5.4**
Total Expenditures	**2,694**	**4,130**	**5,500**	**4.3**	**4.9**	**3.6**

SOURCE: U.S. Department of Health and Human Services, Substance Abuse and Mental Health Services Administration 2001a.

1997 (U.S. Office of National Drug Control Policy 2001b, table 40, 166). Changes in methodology in 1998 prevent comparisons with earlier years.

The Treatment Gap. Those who believe that drug treatment is underfunded often point to a huge "treatment gap," which represents the difference between the number of users estimated to need treatment and the number actually receiving treatment. Indeed, until recently, when the National Drug Control Strategy goals were changed so as to aim only at reducing prevalence of drug use, one of the five goals was to "reduce health and social costs to the public of illegal drug use by reducing the treatment gap" (U.S. Office of National Drug Control Policy 2001b, 7).

The treatment gap is calculated by the federal government's Substance Abuse and Mental Health Services Administration. Treatment need is estimated from National Survey on Drug Use and Health questions indicating if a respondent meets the DSM-IV criteria for dependence or abuse (American Psychiatric Association 1994) or has received treatment at a specialty facility,

TABLE 3-3
ESTIMATED TREATMENT GAP, 1995–2001

	Old Method				New Method	
	1995	1996	1997	1998	2000	2001
Needs Treatment (in thousands)	4,646	5,303	5,726	5,031	4,655	6,096
Received Treatment (in thousands)	2,121	1,973	2,137	2,137	774	1,054
Percent Treated	46	37	37	42	17	17
Percent Not Treated	54	63	63	58	83	83
Treatment Gap (in thousands)	2,525	3,330	3,589	2,894	3,881	5,042

SOURCE: U.S. Department of Health and Human Services, Substance Abuse and Mental Health Services Administration, Office of Applied Studies 2002b, 2002c.

meaning a hospital (as an inpatient), a mental health center, or a drug treatment facility.

The current methodology for calculating the treatment gap has been in place only since 2000. From 1991 to 1998, treatment need was determined mainly from National Household Survey on Drug Abuse data on use patterns—how frequently respondents said they used drugs—rather than on indicators of a psychiatric diagnosis of dependence or abuse.[16] Estimates of clients treated were based primarily on facility data, not NHSDA self-reports. As indicated in table 3-3, one result of the methodological change has been a huge decrease in the estimated number of users receiving treatment and a correspondingly sizable increase in the treatment gap, which was already large to begin with.

By these estimates, the overwhelming majority of those needing treatment are not receiving it. However, it is not clear that these figures provide useful measurements. The NSDUH does not survey most of the nation's heaviest users and therefore cannot provide a reliable measure of those who are most in need of treatment. It may not even provide a reliable measure of trends in treatment need; the drop in estimated need from 1997 to 1998 (12 percent), and the increase from 2000 to 2001 (31 percent) are implausible, probably merely the consequence of changes in questionnaire design and administration.

Two other, more concrete problems suggest the gaps are overstated. First, the calculations assume that treatment should be available for all those who *need* it, rather than all those who *seek* it. Most of those currently not in treatment are not seeking it, either. And a large and growing share of all treatment-seeking is involuntary, resulting from referrals by the criminal justice system. The treatment gap is often presented or interpreted as indicating a huge unfulfilled demand for treatment; while there are waiting lists for many individual programs, that is not what the gap measures.

The second problem is that over half of those classified as being in need of treatment are users only of marijuana. There is no question that frequent marijuana use generates dependence in many users, and that dependence creates substantial problems. But there is a dearth of evidence showing that treatment for marijuana dependence is effective. Meanwhile, the gap is deflated by the admission to treatment of numerous marijuana arrestees who do not have a serious drug problem but rather are attempting to deal with their current legal problem by entering treatment instead of being processed in court. Even so, that accounts for fewer than 200,000 individuals, a small share of the estimated marijuana treatment gap.

Regardless of whether the treatment gap is overstated, there is a good argument to be made that the concept itself is fundamentally flawed. The treatment gap takes a homogenous view of drug users needing treatment, making no distinction between, say, a criminally active crack addict and a gainfully employed computer programmer with a marijuana habit. But the behavior of these users differs so greatly, as does the social value of getting each of them into treatment programs, that it makes no sense to lump them together in a single national measure of treatment adequacy. The formally estimated treatment gap may be a useful political tool to increase funding for treatment, but it arguably diverts attention from the far more important issue of what kind of treatment is being delivered to heavy users of cocaine, crack, and heroin.

This is not to say that there is no treatment gap. Many individual programs report waiting lists, and having to wait even a few weeks has high costs because the untreated addict is frequently such a high-rate offender, and because by the time a slot is available the desire for treatment may have passed. Yet few cities have integrated information systems that allow them to direct patients to the nearest available facility with an opening. Some evidence for unmet demand can be found in Baltimore, a city with a particularly severe heroin problem. A combination of government and private funds has led to a large expansion in treatment capacity; whereas in 1997 11,000 persons were in treatment, by 2003 the total was 24,000 (unpublished data from the Maryland Bureau of Substance Abuse Services); and yet waiting lines do not seem to have declined over that period.

Managed Care. In what may prove to be a critical development in drug treatment, corporations, private health insurers, Medicaid, and other government payers are rapidly adopting managed care arrangements for the provision of drug abuse services. In 1999, 54.2 percent of treatment providers reporting to the Uniform Facility Data Set had managed care contracts, compared to 32.3 percent in 1995. States increasingly "carve out" mental health care and substance abuse treatment from their Medicaid programs, transferring management responsibility (and sometimes financial risk) to other public or private entities (U.S. Department of Health and Human Services, Substance Abuse and Mental Health Services Administration 2001a). The hope, of course, is that managed care will improve the efficiency of treatment spending, as it has, to some degree, in other areas of medical care.

There is little question that managed care of substance abuse services has led and will continue to lead to reductions in hospital-based care. In 1997, hospital-based facilities garnered 38 percent of total drug abuse treatment expenditures, compared to 52 percent a decade earlier. In principle, this is a welcome development. It is widely believed, based on evidence from alcohol treatment and mental health services, that much hospital-based drug treatment is not cost-effective.[17] With alcoholism, a number of researchers have concluded that more expensive hospital-based inpatient treatments are no more effective than other, less expensive treatments (U.S. Congress, Office of Technology Assessment 1983; Miller and Hester 1986). The Institute of Medicine (1990) has estimated that about one-third of inpatient alcohol treatment episodes are inappropriate. In the case of mental health care, evidence suggests that perhaps as many as 40 percent of all psychiatric hospitalizations are inappropriate (Strumwasser et al. 1991). In practice, however, reductions in hospital-based drug treatment may be a problem if eliminated treatment is replaced by less effective care, such as detoxification, arguably an ineffective treatment modality (Thompson et al. 1992).

Managed care is premised on the notion that hospitals, physicians, and service providers respond to financial incentives, and that incentives can be structured to improve the cost-effectiveness of care. Whether that can or will be accomplished with drug treatment remains to be seen. Evidence to date from state Medicaid programs is mixed. Massachusetts, for example, significantly reduced costs while, on some measures, improving overall access to treatment (Callahan et al. 1995). But in Michigan, another state that carved out substance abuse treatment from Medicaid, savings were achieved primarily by reducing the number of clients served rather than by reducing treatment costs per client (Hodgkin et al. 2004).

Prevention

Prevention programs, aimed at reducing experimentation and occasional drug use primarily by children and adolescents, enjoy strong support across the political spectrum. There is no controversy about the desirability of the goal. There is, however, huge disagreement about how best to achieve it, in particular with respect to the role of the most popular prevention program, Drug Abuse Resistance Education (DARE).

The vast majority of drug users begin using some drug before the age of eighteen. Schools constitute the only institutional setting in which most individuals under eighteen can be reached by a program rather than a brief message. Hence, the focus of drug prevention has been on school-based programs; the single largest federal program is the Safe and Drug-Free Schools and Community Act, which disburses about $600 million annually to schools. What follows is a brief summary of the major prevention efforts.

DARE. In 1983 the Los Angeles police chief, Daryl Gates, launched a program in which police officers gave regularly scheduled classes to children in fifth and sixth grades aimed at persuading them to avoid use of illicit drugs. The program was declared to have very high success rates, reducing drug use by age sixteen substantially. A national DARE office was created to expand the program across the entire nation. Congress, subject to considerable lobbying, set aside funds for schools to purchase DARE services from police departments. Teachers supported the program, which relieved them of a burdensome responsibility and allowed them more time for preparation of other classes.

By 1995, DARE had been adopted by many school districts. The National Study of Delinquency Prevention survey of schools in the year 2000 found that 48 percent of elementary schools used some form of DARE, compared to no more than 5 percent for the next-most-popular program (Gottfredson et al. 2000).

Repeated evaluations, however, have found DARE to be ineffective in meeting its stated goal: reduction in the prevalence of drug use (Gottfredson et al. 2002). The program's main achievement may have been increased adolescent trust of police—a not insubstantial gain if it was achieved. Yet even if true, that should not allow DARE to fly under the flag of drug prevention.

In 2001, after fiercely rejecting all the negative evaluations as either methodologically flawed or irrelevant because they assessed dated versions of the program, the national DARE office agreed that its current program was not effective. The change was striking, because the program had vilified a number of researchers who had produced those negative evaluations. With a large grant from the Robert Wood Johnson Foundation, DARE has now launched a five-year national evaluation, conducted by independent experts. The program will still be built around putting police officers in classrooms. However, the messages themselves will be revised to reflect recent advances in understanding of the principles of effective prevention. One clear message from the research is that effective prevention is not taught directly by instructors, but comes from more interactive learning processes. DARE may not be the best platform for doing this, but it is already in so many schools that it may be more sensible to redesign the program than to build something entirely new that will have to prove itself to those schools.

Other School Programs. Parental concern about adolescent drug use has spawned a vast array of prevention programs for schools. One sample of 1,279 schools reported 139 different prevention programs, covering both drugs and other delinquencies (Gottfredson et al. 2000). Most of them were locally developed, and literally nothing is known about how well they work. Most are probably adaptations of one of the well-known national programs, but the adaptation may be so substantial that there is little basis for believing the local version has the same effects. There are enough competing programs that a cottage industry of guidebooks for parents and school districts has sprung up (see, for example, Drug Strategies 1996).

It may well be that a great variety of prevention programs is needed, as schools differ in their populations and in their capacities to deliver such messages. But there is no reason to believe schools are doing a good job of picking the program that is right for their specific needs. Indeed, there is no way that they could do so, given the lack of credible evaluations.

Mass Media. One of the Clinton administration's most visible innovations in drug policy was the funding of a large mass-media campaign in cooperation with the Partnership for a Drug-Free America. Congress appropriated $195 million a year, starting in 1998, which was to be matched by an equal amount from the corporate sector. The antidrug announcements appeared in all the mass media, from full-page ads in major newspapers to public service announcements on prime-time television.

A difficulty for all drug prevention is that antidrug messages have to be heard amid the cacophony of prodrug messages that come from the popular culture. Films like *Trainspotting* and *Pulp Fiction*, though including scenes that show the dangers of drug use, nonetheless provide it with considerable glamour. Antidrug messages, whether presented by the media or in schools, must compete with these.

Secondary and Tertiary Prevention. In the United States, prevention is almost exclusively focused on reducing the number of persons who begin to use drugs, an approach often called primary prevention. Almost no attention is given to desistance programs aimed at identifying and stopping drug use after it has begun but before it has produced identifiable symptoms or problems (secondary prevention). Such programs are found in many other countries; for example, in Edinburgh, an organization called CREW 2000 attempts to reach young people in dance clubs to inform them about the risks of using particular drugs.[18] Nor, except for formal treatment, are there many programs that aim to minimize the health consequences of drug abuse (tertiary prevention); we shall discuss these later under the rubric of harm reduction.

Secondary and tertiary prevention programs may offer substantial benefits, partly because they allow for tighter targeting. While primary prevention may classify children roughly by risk category, in school settings it is hard to deliver anything other than universal messages. Consequently, as is true of prevention in many fields, many resources are spent on low-risk targets (Rose 1992). Secondary prevention programs are better targeted because they aim only at those who actually do begin drug use, although that is hardly a small fraction nowadays. Tertiary prevention, which focuses on problem users, is even more tightly targeted.

4

Policy Effectiveness

Standards of Effectiveness

Our discussion of the effectiveness of American drug policy is deliberately modest. We consider the marginal impact of policies more than the effect of policies in their entirety, and we judge the effectiveness of components of drug policy against one another and not against some absolute standard of public value. Thus, for example, in expressing doubts about the effectiveness of interdiction and offering a more positive assessment of treatment, we are suggesting mainly that reallocating some resources from interdiction to treatment would be beneficial. Completely eliminating interdiction, or raising taxes to expand treatment radically, might be in the national interest, but any such broad conclusions would be highly speculative. Available data tell us relatively little about the likely effects of extensive changes in drug policy, and proposals for making major shifts in overall drug-control spending raise questions about the relative value of drug control and other public policy goals. In any event, there is no serious political consideration of wholesale reform of current drug policy.

This chapter surveys what is known about how well each of the broad classes of programs works. As befits its dominance of drug policy in America, enforcement gets the lion's share of the chapter, although there is less systematic information about its effects than about the effects of treatment and prevention.

Enforcement Effectiveness

It was once widely believed that enforcement reduces drug consumption by limiting the capacity of the illicit drug industry to produce and distribute drugs. According to this view, a kilo of drugs eradicated or seized is a kilo of drugs that is not consumed, and a trafficker or dealer removed or deterred from the drug trade represents one less person delivering drugs to users. Indeed, under federal law, the National Drug Control Strategy must include "an assessment of the reduction of drug availability against an ascertained baseline, as measured by the quantities of cocaine, heroin, marijuana, methamphetamine, and other drugs available for consumption in the United States."[1]

This often-cited measure—the volume of a drug "available for consumption in the United States"—suggests that the main purpose of source-country control is to reduce the volume of drugs available for shipment to the United States, while the function of interdiction is to prevent shipments from entering the country, thus reducing the amount of drugs available for domestic distribution. In turn, domestic seizures are seen as removing additional drug volume from the market, while arrests of traffickers and dealers and confiscation of their assets diminish the capacity of the distribution system, thereby preventing drugs from getting delivered to users. The one major study reflecting this perspective concluded that interdiction is very effective because the volume of seizures per enforcement dollar is higher than for domestic enforcement (Godshaw, Koppell, and Pancoast 1987).

But the idea that crop eradication, seizures, and arrests directly reduce drug consumption ignores the fact that drugs are bought and sold in markets, and that the actors involved respond to economic incentives, which indeed is the notion underlying the separation of programs into "demand reduction" and "supply reduction." On the demand side of the market, enforcement lowers the demand for drugs by incarcerating some users (or forcing them into treatment) and persuading others that it is more difficult and risky for them to buy drugs. On the supply side, enforcement lowers drug use by making drugs more expensive.

Enforcement operations create risks for those in the drug trade—risks of arrest, imprisonment, and the loss of drugs, money, and physical assets. Farmers, smugglers, traffickers, and dealers take steps to reduce the impact of these risks—such as growing or shipping more drugs to make up for losses, or switching to smuggling or distribution methods that are less vulnerable to detection. To compensate for the costs of eradication, seizures, arrests, and efforts to avoid enforcement, farmers, smugglers, and trafficking organizations charge higher prices to downstream distributors and dealers. These higher prices are then passed on to consumers, thereby reducing drug consumption.

How well this works in practice depends on two factors: how effective various types of enforcement are in raising the retail prices of drugs, and how responsive drug consumption is to changes in prices.

Source-Country Control

Coca and opium are grown in poor countries—Bolivia, Colombia, and Peru for coca; Afghanistan, Myanmar, Laos, Mexico, and Colombia for opium—where land and labor are cheap and abundant. The result is that, despite eradication efforts, coca leaf and opium are inexpensive, especially when compared to cocaine and heroin sold at retail. South American coca farmers receive about $300 for the amount of coca leaves necessary to produce a kilogram of cocaine, which retails for about $150,000 in major American cities when sold in $100 units of one gram each, two-thirds pure. A kilogram of raw opium latex sells for as little as $200 in Colombia, the primary source country for heroin imported into the United States (United Nations Office on Drugs and Crime 2003a). When refined, a kilogram of opium produces one hundred grams of heroin, which might generate $50,000 in retail sales.[2] The general pattern of prices increasing sharply through the distribution system is summarized in table 4-1, which provides estimates of the value of a kilogram of pure cocaine (and its earlier forms of leaf and base) at various stages of production and distribution.

These numbers cast serious doubt on the merits of crop eradication as an enforcement strategy. Suppose that stepped-up eradication led to a doubling of the price of coca leaf, so that it cost $600 for refiners to buy the leaf that goes into one kilogram of cocaine. Assuming that the $300 per kilogram cost increase was passed along to traffickers and dealers, the resulting change in the retail price of cocaine would be negligible. In fact, leaf prices in the Andes have increased considerably since the mid-1990s, with no corresponding rise in the retail price of cocaine.

If history is a guide, there appears to be one set of circumstances in which source-country control can produce a meaningful increase in retail

TABLE 4-1
COCAINE PRICES THROUGH THE DISTRIBUTION SYSTEM, 2000

Product	Market Level[a]	Effective Price/kg.
Coca leaves	Farmgate/Colombia	$300
Coca base	Farmgate/Colombia	$900
Cocaine hydrochloride	Export/Colombia	$1,500
Cocaine hydrochloride	Import/U.S. (100kg)	$15,000
Cocaine (67% pure)	Dealer/U.S. (1 kg)	$40,000
Cocaine (67% pure)	Retail/U.S. (200 mg)	$150,000

SOURCE: United Nations Office on Drugs and Crime 2003a, 2004; U.S. Office of National Drug Control Policy 2001d; Reuter and Greenfield 2001.
a. Figures in parentheses represent typical transaction sizes at that market level.

prices and a drop in consumption. Cultivation levels are based on the expectation that a portion of crops will be wiped out, and when eradication destroys a much larger share of crop production than farmers anticipate, a genuine shortage can result. Such a shortage lasts until traffickers find new sources of supply and farmers adapt by increasing the total land area cultivated and by scattering their plants in smaller, less accessible fields. In the interim (perhaps six months to three years), consumption falls, and prices rise as users compete for a diminished supply.

Crop eradication has had a significant impact on U.S. drug consumption only in the 1970s. In the early part of the 1970s, the Turkish opium ban (combined with the breaking of the "French connection") produced a substantial shortage of heroin on the East Coast of the United States, which lasted for two to three years until imports from Mexico and Asia picked up the slack. As discussed in the previous chapter, a major heroin shortage again developed in the mid- to late-1970s, as the Mexican government engaged in widespread aerial spraying of poppy fields. Mexican opium production fell by about 75 percent, and there was a significant decline over four years (1976–79) in indicators of U.S. heroin consumption, particularly in areas of the country where Mexican "black tar" was the predominant type of heroin used.

However, if we look more closely at these experiences, it becomes clear that such successes will be rare. In both situations, the relevant source country was by far the largest supplier to the U.S. market (Reuter

1985). And the resulting reductions in drug cultivation were massive—at least 50 percent and possibly much more. Furthermore, the control programs were sudden, almost out-of-the-blue moves, rather than moderate escalations of existing crop-control efforts.

Equally important were the political and economic circumstances that enabled the central governments involved to undertake such bold action. The authority of the Turkish and Mexican governments was largely unchallenged in the growing areas—something that cannot be said about Afghanistan, Colombia, or Myanmar today. And in both Turkey and Mexico, revenues from drug production and trafficking were, by the standards of other major source countries, only a small part of national and regional economies.

Interdiction

Bogotá is approximately 1,500 miles from Miami; Miami is roughly 2,700 miles from Seattle. Yet the difference between wholesale cocaine prices in Miami and Seattle is very small compared to the tenfold difference between wholesale prices in Bogotá and Miami. It is clear that interdiction imposes significant costs on cocaine smuggling, and that these costs have a significant effect on the import price of cocaine in the United States. International borders represent locations where the government has unique authority to search and inspect; they are more dangerous for smugglers than any other place.

But that fact does not mean interdiction is a particularly effective policy for reducing the consumption of drugs. The key issue is how changes in the import price of drugs affect retail prices. Let's say a kilogram of cocaine sells for $15,000 at import in Miami and $150,000 at retail in New York. Now imagine that more effective interdiction boosts the import price to $30,000. How would this affect the retail price of cocaine?

This question is a crucial one, because the answer determines the ultimate value of the enhanced interdiction efforts. One theory of vertical price relationships, which Caulkins (1990) has termed the "additive model," argues that the import price is essentially a raw material cost (Reuter and Kleiman 1986). Thus, the wholesaler who previously bought cocaine at

$15,000 and now pays $30,000 has had roughly $15,000 added to his per-kilo costs. The actual cost increase will be somewhat more than $15,000 per kilo; due to seizures, thefts, and other losses, wholesalers have to buy more than one kilo of drug for each kilo they sell.

In a competitive market, the wholesaler will simply pass his increased costs along to the next stage of the distribution chain. The buyer at this stage will thus face an increase of $15,000 in his costs, which he, too, will pass along. Eventually, the $15,000 cost increase reaches consumers, and the end result is that the retail price of cocaine increases by $15 per gram—or somewhat more, when all the losses and seizures along the distribution chain are factored in. Analysts at the RAND Corporation have estimated that, for cocaine and marijuana, each $1 increase in the import price produces a $2 increase in retail prices (Reuter, Crawford, and Cave 1988).[3] Overall, then, a doubling of the import price results in only a 10 or 20 percent rise in the retail price. Or, put another way, it would take a quintupling of import prices to effect a doubling of retail prices.

Most of the few empirical analyses of interdiction have assumed the additive model. And because the replacement cost of seized cocaine and heroin is a small fraction of their final retail price—as little as 1 percent in source countries, no more than 20 percent at the point of entry into the United States—these analyses have concluded that the potential contribution of interdiction to the reduction of drug abuse is small, or at least that it is not cost-effective compared to domestic enforcement and treatment (Rydell and Everingham 1994).

Although the additive model is conceptually compelling—no one would dispute it in the case of a licit industry—some scholars have noted that it does not fit very well with some historical price data (see Boyum 1992 and Caulkins 1990). In fact, some historical price data appear to be more consistent with what Caulkins has called the "multiplicative model" of vertical price relationships, which holds that a change of a certain percentage in price at one stage of production or distribution brings about a similar percentage change at subsequent stages. The idea behind the multiplicative model is that many of the costs of doing business in the drug trade—such as the risk of employees and other dealers stealing drugs—are more strongly related to the value of drugs bought and sold than to the quantity trafficked. Thus, the multiplicative model predicts that if the import price of cocaine doubles from $15,000 to $30,000, retail prices will also double, from $150,000 to $300,000, providing a much more favorable assessment of interdiction.

Jonathan Caulkins examined cocaine prices in the 1980s and early 1990s and found a remarkably consistent multiplicative relationship between wholesale and retail prices. However, the data supporting a multiplicative model were far from conclusive. The trouble here was that, except during occasional shortages, prices were consistently declining during this period, and so it is possible that the factors causing the decline operated at all levels of the market. In other words, it may be that declines in retail prices were not so much caused by the decline in import prices, but rather that both import and retail prices were influenced by other factors. For example, the growth in the cocaine industry internationally, and the development of crack markets domestically, may have created economies of scale that lowered the costs of both wholesale and retail operations.

In short, the nature of vertical price relationships in drug markets is still an open question. And it is, of course, possible that the answer lies somewhere in between the additive and multiplicative models. Indeed, some have speculated that the multiplicative model may hold for retail transactions, but that the additive model may apply for higher-level wholesale transactions (Boyum 1993; Caulkins 1990).

Summing up, it is clear that interdiction imposes considerable costs on drug traffickers. Import prices are much higher than they would be if American borders were unpoliced. What is not clear is whether interdiction adds more than 10 or 20 percent to the retail price of drugs; data are inconclusive. What is also uncertain is whether sizable increases or decreases in the interdiction budget have more than a negligible effect on retail drug prices. It may be that a 50 percent reduction in interdiction funding would be inconsequential because the remaining seizure effort would be sufficient to prompt traffickers to take costly avoidance actions. In any case, given that standard economic reasoning casts suspicion on interdiction, and bearing in mind the paucity of evidence linking shifts in the intensity of interdiction to observed changes in retail drug prices (except, possibly, for marijuana), the case for more expenditure on interdiction should be considered unproven, at least at current levels of activity.

Domestic Enforcement

Domestic enforcement makes a major contribution to reducing the consumption of drugs. About 90 percent of the retail price of cocaine and heroin represents price markups within the United States. One major reason that low-level enforcement has a great influence on drug prices as compared to interdiction or enforcement against high-level dealers is that the risks of incarceration are distributed over much smaller quantities of drugs; the retailer handling a gram of cocaine faces a prison sentence that might be one-quarter of that faced by a high-level dealer handling 1,000 grams, so the expected prison time per gram is higher for retailers. In the absence of domestic enforcement, these drugs would be considerably cheaper.[4] While there is some debate about how responsive drug consumption is to changes in prices, most recent studies indicate it is highly price-sensitive. Based on the research, it would be reasonable to assume, for example, that, other things being equal, a 50 percent decline in cocaine prices would double overall consumption (Caulkins and Reuter 1998). Note that a doubling of consumption does not mean a doubling in the number of users; much of the increased use would be accounted for by greater consumption per existing user.

Domestic enforcement also reduces drug consumption by directly lowering demand. Since most drug sellers are also users, the incarceration of sellers reduces the number of active buyers. And some kinds of enforcement also lower demand by threatening buyers with arrest and otherwise making it harder for them to find safe and easily accessible buying opportunities.

While it is clear that domestic drug enforcement has kept prices much higher than they would be in the absence of enforcement, it is not evident that the massive increase in enforcement over the past two decades has had much impact on prices. Figure 4-1 contrasts the retail price of cocaine per pure gram (adjusted for inflation and expressed in 2000 dollars) with a rough measure of the law enforcement risk facing cocaine dealers: the number of heroin and cocaine arrests (state and local data do not, unfortunately, distinguish them) for each $1 million in cocaine sales (also in 2000 dollars). The chart indicates that from 1981 to 2000, a more than tenfold increase in enforcement pressure—most of which occurred during the 1980s—was accompanied by a two-thirds decline in the retail price of cocaine. And the estimated increase in enforcement

FIGURE 4-1

RETAIL COCAINE PRICE VS. ARRESTS PER $1 MILLION IN
COCAINE SALES, 1981–2000

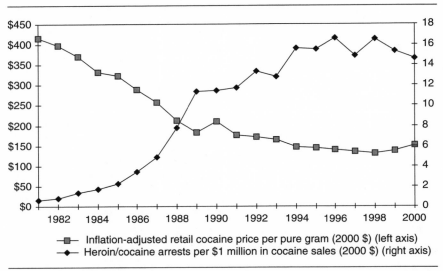

SOURCE: Rydell and Everingham 1994; U.S. Office of National Drug Control Policy 2001a, 2001c.

pressure would probably be even greater than shown if the severity of punishment per arrest was considered. Over the course of the 1980s, the percentage of drug arrests that led to incarceration also rose sharply.

Why cocaine prices fell precipitously in the face of such increased punishment for drug law violations is something of a puzzle, although the fact that dealers removed from the trade are easily replaced is surely part of the story. But whatever the explanation, the trends warrant greater skepticism about the ability of more intense enforcement to reduce consumption by boosting prices. Moreover, drug enforcement presumably exhibits diminishing marginal returns. It induces traffickers and dealers to take steps to avoid detection, which then makes it more difficult for additional enforcement to pressure them.

It is plausible, then, that the first 20 percent of our enforcement effort accounts for most of the effect of enforcement on drug prices. If this is the case, then even a sharp reduction in arrests or a substantial shortening of sentences might result in only a small decline in prices. Kuziemko and Levitt

(2004) and Bushway, Caulkins, and Reuter (2003), using statistical models, have found, at most, very modest effects of tougher state and local enforcement on retail cocaine prices.

Yet the effectiveness of domestic enforcement cannot be judged solely by its impact on drug prices and consumption. Large criminal enterprises are heavily involved in domestic drug distribution. Reducing the size and wealth of such organizations, and in turn their capacity to corrupt law enforcement and use drug profits to finance other criminal activities, might be an important aim of domestic drug enforcement, independent of any effect on prices and consumption. Much of the work of the federal Drug Enforcement Administration, and a small but not insignificant share of FBI activity, consists of high-level enforcement focused on dismantling large drug-trafficking organizations.

However, the illicit drug industry may have adapted in ways that make it more resilient in the face of such enforcement efforts. Forty years ago, the American Mafia—an organization whose membership and boundaries were easily defined—dominated high-level heroin dealing. Today, drug-trafficking organizations are less well-defined and less stable. With the exception of certain gangs operating in retail dealing, most organizations today resemble a confederation or network of freelance traffickers or small trafficking groups more than a single, tight-knit, organization.[5] Fuentes (1998) has described two very large Colombian cocaine-importing organizations with hundreds of employees that existed in New York in the early 1990s, but these seem to have been an exception.

A networked structure of distributors makes it more difficult to bring down a major part of a drug-distribution system. If a large section of a traditional organized-crime group is dismantled, others within that organization may be unable to function; indeed, the federal government's anti-Mafia efforts of the 1980s and 1990s constitute a major success story (Reuter 1995). In today's drug-trafficking environment, traffickers at all levels are likely to work with several groups, both above and below them in the distribution chain, so that the loss of one set of connections is a less serious blow.

Like high-level enforcement, retail- or street-level enforcement also cannot be assessed simply by the yardstick of consumption. Retail markets for cocaine, heroin, and methamphetamine often generate high levels of violence, disorder, and community fear, and lure large numbers of poor (and typically minority) youths away from education and legitimate employment. Insofar as street-level enforcement can beneficially influence the distribution and character of retail drug markets—by limiting flagrant and violent dealing and reducing the flow of youths into the drug trade—it can substantially improve conditions in drug-involved neighborhoods.

The success of street-level enforcement varies greatly on this score, even within cities. Crackdowns designed to produce large numbers of dealer arrests and seizures are a common response to retail drug markets, but they rarely work well as a long-term strategy. Crackdowns are difficult to sustain, can intensify violent competition among dealers, and may result in the replacement of older dealers with younger, more violent ones.[6] What appears most effective is a shift away from the traditional approach of simply seizing drugs and arresting dealers toward a strategy of selective market disruption (U.S. Department of Justice, National Institute of Justice, Office of Justice Programs 1993b).

The idea of selective market disruption is to pick out especially violent or neighborhood-disrupting segments of the drug market in an area—particular drugs, locations, dealing styles, or gangs—and make it difficult for buyers and sellers in those segments to connect. Selective market disruption accepts that law enforcement cannot eliminate entire drug markets; instead, it tries to shape the character of markets by targeting their most damaging aspects.

Particularly important, it appears, is disrupting street markets and moving them indoors, and disrupting "drug-house" markets and pressuring sellers to adopt more discreet dealing strategies. Open street markets present numerous opportunities for conflict and violence—disputes over turf, disputes over customers, disputes between dealers and police, simple robbery. Indoor markets, which are not publicly visible and are easily accessible only to established customers, are less disruptive of neighborhood functioning and less prone to violence. As David Kennedy, a leading advocate of arrest-minimizing enforcement strategies, puts it: "All drug markets present trouble for communities, but street drug markets are the worst trouble of all. Eliminating them would be a huge stride toward quelling drug-related violence and disorder" (U.S. Office of National Drug Control Policy 1994b).

Recent technological changes, in particular the use of cell phones, may considerably reduce the extent of street markets in the future, as buyers and sellers are able to make safe contact before a transaction, reducing the time and risk for both sides. Marijuana markets rarely create these problems, because so many transactions occur in the context of routine social relations.

The effectiveness of domestic enforcement could also be enhanced by reforming sentencing policy. Studies of state prisoners have often shown that a majority of incarcerated drug offenders have no documented history of criminal violence. Sevigny and Caulkins 2004 use a survey of prison inmates to show that most of those locked up are indeed drug dealers, but probably at the low end of the business. Although most have prior convictions, few show any indication of involvement in violent crime. Since their cells could instead be holding more dangerous offenders, long, mandatory sentences for nonviolent drug offenders are arguably counterproductive from a public safety perspective.

User Sanctions

Most discussions and analyses of drug policy focus either on pure supply-side programs, such as enforcement and interdiction, or pure demand-side programs, such as prevention and treatment. There is, however, an additional set of various "crossover" programs that use direct sanctions to discourage drug use. These include arrest and criminal penalties for simple possession; testing for drug use and searching for possession with associated civil penalties in other settings, such as schools and workplaces; denial of benefits and privileges, such as welfare, student loans, or public housing, contingent on conviction for a drug offense; and coerced abstinence, the use of graduated and immediate sanctions for the detection of drug use by an individual under the supervision of the criminal justice system.

Though they seem to have become increasingly common, there has been very little evaluation of any of these drug-control approaches. One program, Transitional Aid for Needy Families (TANF), the successor to Aid to Families with Dependent Children, requires that clients demonstrate abstinence from illicit drugs.[7] In 1996, when TANF was introduced, at least eight states declared their intention to test recipients for recent drug use and make continued abstinence a condition for continued receipt of benefits (Legal Action Center 1997). Those who tested positive would be required to enter a treatment program or find some alternative means of abstaining. Failure to desist would be grounds for termination. In fact, no state has succeeded in implementing a program of universal testing. Michigan began testing in 1998, but the testing was halted by a federal court order (on civil liberties grounds) within a few weeks. A federal appeals court upheld that decision in April 2003.

Most large companies, and many small ones, require drug tests of job applicants. Some observers believe this has made an important contribution to the reduction in drug use among adults that has occurred since the mid-1980s. Adolescent use rose in the 1990s, but the desistance at an earlier age as compared to the 1970s and early 1980s may reflect increasing concern about the job consequences of using drugs, particularly marijuana, which has a long detection window in urine tests—thirty days, as compared to three days for cocaine.

There is much less evidence to support the notion that random testing of high school and junior high school athletes, along with locker searches, have affected drug use. The rise in adolescent use rates has occurred as more and more schools have implemented such policies, but this is hardly dispositive. Researchers from Monitoring the Future have found no association between school drug-testing policies and the likelihood that students use drugs (Yamaguchi, Johnston, and O'Malley 2003). However, a recent, small-scale study of an Oregon school that aggressively tested found it had drug-use rates only one-quarter those of a comparable school with no drug-testing policy.

The idea of mandating abstinence from drug use among those on probation, parole, and pretrial release, and enforcing that mandate with frequent drug tests accompanied by prompt and predictable sanctions for failed or missed tests, remains promising. Persons under the supervision of the criminal justice system account for the lion's share of cocaine and heroin consumption in volume terms, and drug use, even among this population, is influenced by incentives. But so far only Maryland has advanced the concept of coerced abstinence beyond a pilot program, and the record there and elsewhere suggests that the political and administrative obstacles to implementing a successful program are considerable.

FIGURE 4-2

**PREVALENCE OF WEEKLY COCAINE USE AMONG
DATOS PATIENTS, BEFORE AND AFTER TREATMENT**

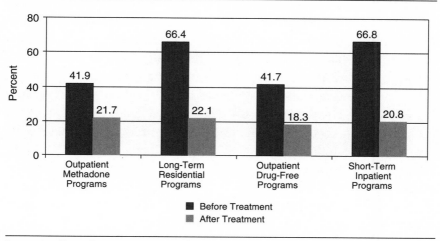

SOURCE: Mueller and Wyman 1997.

Treatment Effectiveness

We can report more detail on treatment effectiveness than we can for enforcement efforts, both because it is easier to do evaluations of individually focused programs and because there has been more pressure on such programs to justify themselves (Reuter 2001). Most studies have found that participation in treatment programs is associated with declines in reported drug use and behavioral problems, both during and after treatment episodes. Consider, for instance, findings from the Drug Abuse Treatment Outcome Study (DATOS)—the largest study of treatment outcomes since the early 1980s— which tracked 10,010 drug users who entered treatment programs between 1991 and 1993. Based on a random sample of approximately 3,000 DATOS patients, figure 4-2 compares reported weekly cocaine use twelve months before treatment with reported weekly use twelve months after completion or discontinuance of treatment, for four different treatment modalities. (Outpatient methadone patients still in treatment were interviewed approximately twenty-four months after admission.)

Data Limitations. For many advocates of increased funding of treatment programs, such before-and-after findings demonstrate that treatment works. "DATOS overwhelmingly confirms the effectiveness of drug abuse treatment," asserted Alan Leshner when he was director of the National Institute on Drug Abuse. "Among the patients that DATOS studied, drug use dropped significantly from the 12 months before treatment to 12 months after treatment began" (Leshner 1997). But while it may be reasonable to conclude that treatment is effective in reducing drug use, such simple before-and-after comparisons are inadequate to make the case. Because DATOS was an observational study that did not employ properly selected control groups—that is, samples of similar drug users who did not receive treatment—it is difficult to know how much, if any, improved behavior among treatment participants is attributable to treatment as opposed to other factors.

For example, a small part of the improvement may be due to aging, since most heavy drug users and many heavy alcohol users outgrow their habits over time. A bigger issue is self-selection. Heavy users generally enter treatment programs when their up-and-down cycle of substance abuse and behavioral problems is at a peak (Anglin and Hser 1990). Thus, subsequent reductions in substance abuse and associated problems may in part represent a regression to the mean. Other selection bias is also possible: for reasons other than regression effects, drug users who voluntarily or involuntarily enter treatment may be more "ready" to quit than other users, and therefore more likely than other users to desist in the absence of treatment.

The standard approach for controlling for such confounding effects is the randomized clinical trial, in which subjects are randomly assigned either to receive the intervention under investigation or to be given a placebo. Because randomization ensures that the treatment and control groups are roughly similar, apart from having received the intervention or the placebo, any differences in results between the two groups can be attributed to the intervention.

A barrier to randomized clinical trials of drug treatment interventions is that many consider it unethical to deny treatment to a placebo group of addicted users, treatment being the accepted therapy for addiction. Partly as a result, there have been, unfortunately, few randomized clinical trials of drug treatment interventions, a problem to which the National Research

Council's Committee on Data and Research for Policy on Illegal Drugs recently called attention (Manski, Pepper, and Petrie 2001, 263). The NRC committee also criticized researchers for what it saw as excessive reliance on findings from DATOS and similar uncontrolled studies.

Yet randomized trials can still be used to compare different modalities for individuals receiving treatment intervention. For example, randomized trials strongly support high methadone dosages in improving retention and in reducing opiate use (Faggiano et al. 2004). More to the point, the fact that most treatment research has been flawed, and that many have read too much into the results of less-than-definitive research, does not mean that next to nothing can be inferred from existing research about the effectiveness of treatment. Policymakers are particularly interested in the relative benefits and costs of treatment compared to prevention, interdiction, domestic enforcement, and other antidrug interventions, as well as the relative cost-effectiveness of treatment compared to alternative policy choices. In light of the limitations of treatment research, the NRC committee concluded: "At present, there is little firm basis for estimating the benefit-cost ratio or relative cost-effectiveness of drug treatment" (Manski, Pepper, and Petrie 2001, 244). This is, in our view, a substantial overstatement of the level of ignorance. Despite real and perhaps inherent imprecision of program evaluation and policy analysis in this area, the pattern of available data and findings has clear and robust implications for the allocation of public resources.

What Is Known about Treatment Effectiveness. Methadone maintenance has proved more effective than other treatment approaches at reducing heroin use and criminal activity in a number of randomized clinical trials (see, for example, Sees et al. 2000). Further evidence of the efficacy of methadone comes from randomized trials comparing different dosages; findings strongly support high dosages in improving retention and in reducing opiate use (see, for example, Strain et al. 1999). Other opioid agonists (substitutes)—levo-alpha-acetyl-methadol (LAAM) and buprenorphine—have also shown positive outcomes in randomized clinical trials (Johnson et al. 2000), as have opioid-antagonist medications, such as naltrexone, that block the effects of heroin (Cornish et al. 1997).

Various pieces of evidence also suggest that aging, regression to the mean, and other selection effects cannot fully account for the reduction in drug use observed among treatment participants. In the initial years of the California Civil Addict Program (CAP), which began in 1961, about half of CAP clients were discharged from treatment shortly after admission because of legal or procedural errors in their commitments. Both those discharged and those who stayed showed significant reductions in drug use and crime from their immediate preadmission levels (suggesting aging and regression to the mean effects), but the clients who remained in the CAP had about half the level of drug use and criminal activity of the discharged group (McGlothlin, Anglin, and Wilson 1977).

Other studies indicate that those who are coerced into nonprison treatment by the criminal justice system fare as well as, if not better than, those who enter such programs voluntarily (Anglin and Hser 1990). In addition, longitudinal studies of drug treatment consistently have shown that drug use rises following termination of outpatient treatment, which would not be expected if the treatment had no impact on drug use (Hubbard et al. 1989).

There are also methods of analyzing data from major longitudinal studies of drug treatment that are likely to lessen the confounding effects of selection bias. In a highly publicized study that evaluated the cost-effectiveness of four types of cocaine-control policies—source-country control, interdiction, domestic enforcement, and treatment of heavy users—RAND estimated the effects of treatment by comparing clients whose treatment lasted less than three months with clients whose treatment lasted three months or longer (Rydell and Everingham 1994).[8] Although it is plausible that those who drop (or are kicked) out of treatment programs shortly after entering are less disciplined, motivated, or otherwise amenable to treatment than those who stay in longer, RAND's approach should at least partly eliminate bias from selection effects. Indeed, the methodology is conservative in the sense that any effect of treatment interventions lasting less than three months is not counted.

The RAND study, *Controlling Cocaine: Supply Versus Demand Programs*, estimated that each dollar spent on treatment reduces the costs of crime and lost productivity by $7.46. By contrast, none of the supply-control interventions broke even. In total social benefits and cost savings, source-country control was estimated to return fifteen cents on the dollar, interdiction thirty-two cents, and domestic enforcement fifty-two cents.[9] Some have concluded that the uncertainty in these findings renders them worthless. The NRC committee, for example, declared "that the findings lack sufficient persuasiveness to be used as a basis for policy formation" (Manski, Pepper, and Thomas, 1999).

But drug policymakers have to make choices, even when there is great uncertainty as to the costs and benefits of different alternatives. As former treasury secretary Robert Rubin (1999) has noted, "In the end, all decisions are based on imperfect or incomplete information. But decisions must be made—and on a timely basis—whether in school, on the trading floor, or in the White House." Common sense says that those decisions should be made on the basis of the best available evidence, and despite its limitations, the RAND study is the most thorough analysis of alternative cocaine-control policies to date.[10] The NRC committee did not claim there was any systematic bias in the RAND findings, nor did the committee suggest what research or information policymakers should use in lieu of the RAND study. It is also striking that in the ten years since the RAND study appeared, despite the criticism and praise it has received, no other research effort has attempted to answer the same broad question: What is a reasonable way to allocate drug-control resources at the margin?

Moreover, if one looks at the benefit-cost ratios cited above, it is clear that the RAND analysis could be off by a wide margin without changing its fundamental conclusion: that treatment of heavy users is a far more cost-effective policy at the margin than any kind of enforcement. Even if RAND overestimated the benefits of marginal spending on treating heavy users by a factor of three and underestimated the benefits from additional spending on domestic enforcement expenditures by the same margin, an additional dollar spent on treating heavy users would still yield greater social benefit than the same dollar spent on domestic enforcement.

While the RAND study focused on the treatment of heavy cocaine users, analyses have also concluded that methadone maintenance therapy is highly cost-effective in treating heroin users. In fact, because of the high rates of HIV infection among heroin users, methadone maintenance therapy has been shown to be cost-effective even when evaluated solely as an HIV prevention measure (Zaric, Barnett, and Brandeau 2000; Pollack 2001b).

Targeting Heavy Users. Much discussion of treatment focuses on its success or failure in producing abstinence from drug use. Treatment is generally defined as successful if a subject is completely abstinent one year after treatment. Evaluated in this way, most treatment fails as often as or more often than it succeeds. For instance, in the Treatment Outcome Prospective Study (the data from which were used in the RAND study mentioned earlier), one-year abstinence rates among regular cocaine users who stayed in treatment for at least three months ranged from 40 to 47 percent, depending on treatment modality (Hubbard et al. 1989). But it turns out that treatment of heavy, criminally active users can be highly beneficial even if it has no lasting effect on drug use. The most comprehensive treatment research indicates that most of the reduction in criminal activity related to treatment occurs during treatment. Indeed, a crucial finding of the RAND study was that treatment reduces the criminal activity of heavy users during treatment by more than enough to justify its cost, even assuming no effect on posttreatment behavior. Moreover, the trajectory from dependence to abstinence may require several treatment episodes, so a specific course of treatment may reduce the time to ultimate sobriety even if it does not halt drug use in the short term.

Again, the RAND study evaluated the benefits that would come from additional expenditures on treating *heavy* users. But it should not be assumed that additional expenditures on drug treatment would necessarily be directed at the heaviest users. Many treatment providers steer clear of criminally active offenders, who are viewed as poor candidates for program completion and long-term abstinence; the rewards for the program operators relate to the number of patients completing the program, regardless of how much harm they were causing when enrolled. Drug court programs, whose purpose is to divert drug-involved offenders into treatment programs, reinforce this bias. Offenders with a history of violence are typically deemed ineligible for diversion programs, and the criteria used to judge client suitability often discriminate against the heaviest users. Many drug courts refuse to allow clients to remain in methadone programs, despite their proven efficacy.

Also, the availability of methadone maintenance and opiate-replacement therapy is limited not only by funding constraints but by federal regulations, which restrict the care of opioid-dependent patients to federally licensed narcotic treatment programs. Institute of Medicine and National Institutes of Health panels have recommended regulatory reform that would allow heroin addicts to receive treatment in primary care settings (Rettig and Yarmolinsky 1995; National Consensus Development Panel on Effective Medical Treatment of Opiate Addiction 1998). Small studies have found that heroin-dependent patients fare just as well when treated with methadone or buprenorphine in primary care settings as in licensed narcotic treatment programs (Fiellin et al. 2001; O'Connor et al. 1998). Giving treatment in doctors' offices liberates some patients from the dreary clinic environment and, it has been argued, may allow them to avoid the behavioral cues for drug use that surround conventional treatment facilities.

Thus, regulatory reform may be the most cost-effective way to expand available treatment for heroin abusers. The proliferation of buprenorphine may also help here. Buprenorphine is probably less effective than high-dose methadone maintenance therapy in reducing drug use, but buprenorphine is less controversial politically, has lower risk for abuse and dependence and fewer side effects, and its benefits last longer.

Prevention Effectiveness

In the past fifteen years, a substantial research literature has provided insight into the components of effective prevention programs. Simply providing information to people on the dangers of drug use, the basic strategy of the 1970s, has been shown to be ineffective. The same is true of programs that rely on "fear arousal," stressing the dangers of drug use; "moral education," which stresses the evils of drug use; and "affective education," which focuses on building self-esteem, responsible decision making, and interpersonal growth (Manski, Pepper, and Petrie 2001, 223). Individual programs with the best results pay attention to the social context of drug use, which is related to many other aspects of the individual's life and setting. They also involve highly interactive learning. But whether such programs can work on a national scale is unclear.

A few research-based programs have shown promise in large-scale trials (Manski, Pepper, and Petrie 2001), but none has been shown to be effective when implemented without researcher supervision. A recent study concluded that, generally, "Individual prevention activities are not being implemented with sufficient strength and fidelity to be expected to produce a measurable difference in the desired outcomes" (Gottfredson et al. 2000, 10). In other words, programs aren't doing what they're supposed to be doing, so we shouldn't expect them to be effective.

School-Based Programs. To date, few school-based programs have been able to show they are effective. In 2000, an expert panel created by the Department of Education reported on "exemplary" or "promising" programs for drug and violence prevention. It published, after lengthy deliberations, a careful specification of criteria for judging the programs. The panel received 132 submissions of programs seeking these ratings. Only nine received the "exemplary" label, and another thirty-three were classified as "promising." DARE was classified as neither exemplary nor promising.

Of the nine exemplary programs, only two were drug prevention programs aimed at a broad base of students. The others mostly dealt with special populations, such as school athletes, or with just cigarettes and alcohol. At present, there simply is little basis for schools to make decisions about which drug prevention programs to adopt.

One problem is the inherent challenge of implementing relatively subtle programs in the context of poorly managed schools that serve the populations at highest risk of serious drug problems, many of whose students drop out. Another difficulty is that drug prevention is probably best seen as embedded in programs that have broader goals; marijuana prevention, for instance, may be accomplished by interventions that aim at improving student health behavior generally. It is even possible that drug prevention should be treated primarily as a component of classroom management. If teachers manage to keep a well-organized classroom in which students find it easy to learn, drug use may be reduced (Botvin and Botvin 1997). Conversely, drug prevention programs, even if well designed and delivered, may have limited effectiveness if children spend their time in undisciplined and chaotic classrooms.

Frustrated with schools' limited enthusiasm for delivering drug prevention programs consistently or intensively, many community coalitions have tried to develop prevention programs for other settings, such as recreational centers or churches. These are even more difficult to evaluate than school-based programs, and little is known about their effectiveness.

Mass Media. There is a longstanding skepticism about mass-media campaigns to prevent drug use. They easily lend themselves to ridicule, as in the "This is your brain on drugs" ad of the late 1980s. More recently, ONDCP's National Youth Anti-Drug Media Campaign ran ads that announced, on the basis of the most slender of connections, that to buy drugs is to support international terrorism aimed at America. The Partnership for a Drug-Free America, the long-time collaborator with the Office of National Drug Control Policy in such campaigns, considered the ads off-target (Eddy 2003).

Nonetheless, in an age of mass-media campaigns on many issues, including antismoking, these drug prevention efforts cannot be summarily dismissed. ONDCP, mindful of that skepticism, put into place an elaborate evaluation effort for its campaign, though it was inherently difficult to evaluate given precisely that the campaign aimed to reach such a broad audience. An ongoing evaluation sponsored by the National Institute on Drug Abuse has found that the campaign did, indeed, reach the intended target audiences of parents and children. However, the evaluation has found no evidence that exposure changes attitudes toward drugs, let alone drug use, among children: "Youth who were more exposed to Campaign messages are no more likely to hold favorable beliefs or intentions about marijuana than are youth less exposed to those messages" (U.S. Department of Health and Human Services, National Institute on Drug Abuse 2003). Another report even found some reverse effects, with attitudes actually worsening (Hornik et al. 2002).

Perhaps the most promising evidence in favor of mass-media drug prevention is that a number of mass-media campaigns appear to have been effective in reducing youth smoking (Farrelly, Fergusson, and Horwood 2003). The most prominent of these mass media efforts has been the "truth" campaign, which was established under the terms of a 1998 settlement between four tobacco companies and the forty-six states that had sued them. However, many of the antitobacco spots have built on the risk-seeking, countercultural aspects of teenage life. For example, one ad shows a teenager getting a tongue stud in a dingy piercing parlor. The piercer, an older man with decaying teeth, offers the teenager a cigarette. The kid immediately declines, sneering, "What, do think I'm crazy?" It is hard to imagine similar ads coming from the powers-that-be at ONDCP or the Partnership for a Drug-Free America.

Cost-Effectiveness of Prevention. Prevention programs implicitly assume that reducing early drug initiation—the usual measure of effectiveness applied to such programs—will prevent future addiction and crime. This may be true, but one has to wonder whether programs aimed at the entire child and adolescent population are an efficient way to reach the small minority who will become heavy users and account for the vast majority of drug-related harm.

With rare exceptions, the focus of drug prevention evaluations has simply been on effectiveness—whether programs reduce drug use. There has been scant attention to the question more relevant to policy: Are prevention programs worth their cost? A study of this matter authored by Caulkins and RAND collaborators was entitled *An Ounce of Prevention, a Pound of Uncertainty* (1999), reflecting the authors' frustration with the difficulty of pinning down any useful estimates of costs.

According to this study, even best-practice prevention programs would be only about as cost-effective as typical enforcement efforts in reducing cocaine consumption, and far less cost-effective than ordinary drug treatment programs. That's hardly a favorable assessment, and it may well be optimistic. The RAND study estimated the costs of programs in terms of materials, teacher time, and facility costs. Yet that approach leaves out the potentially significant educational cost of having children spend time in drug prevention sessions instead of studying English, math, and other academic subjects.

5

Policy Reform

There is considerable uncertainty about the effectiveness of American drug policy. Indeed, one can reasonably say that choices are driven mostly by images and beliefs. Part of the problem is that relevant data are limited and unreliable. Drug prohibition and enforcement discourage the production, distribution, and use of drugs, but at the same time foster the concealment of these activities, making it hard to collect timely and dependable information about them. We will never know as much about illicit drug use as we do about alcohol and tobacco use.[1]

In addition, drug use is heavily influenced by forces other than drug policy, not least by changing attitudes about drug use and by volatile swings in the fashionability of specific drugs. This inevitably complicates efforts to assess the effects of different policy actions; good policies that face headwinds in attitudes and fashions appear ineffective, while bad policies that enjoy tailwinds look successful. Still another difficulty is that the overall impact of certain components of the nation's drug policy may be dominated by unintended side effects, such as black market violence or foster-child placements resulting from the jailing of low-level female drug dealers. Such side effects are notoriously hard to gauge.

But despite its imperfections, the evidence regarding the effectiveness of drug policy is still meaningful. And the bulk of that evidence points to the same conclusion: As currently implemented, American drug policies are unconvincing. They are intrusive, as illustrated by the prevalence of drug testing of student athletes; divisive, because of the disproportionate share of the burdens (both of drug abuse and of drug control) borne by minority communities; and expensive, with an approximate $35 billion annual expenditure on drug control. And yet they leave the nation with a massive drug problem, greater than that of any other Western nation.

It is possible that U.S. drug policy has done a yeoman's job of curtailing drug abuse, but the evidence is hardly supportive. The marked and steady decline in heroin and cocaine prices in the face of a stepped-up enforcement effort that has placed over 400,000 Americans behind bars suggests that supply-reduction efforts are unable to reduce drug use by further boosting prices. The number of problematic drug users—those with expensive and dangerous cocaine and heroin habits—has declined only modestly over the past ten years. Drug treatment, which, according to the most thorough cost-benefit analyses, is far more effective than enforcement in reducing drug consumption, has received barely 15 percent of federal drug-control spending in recent years, and an even lower percentage if state and local expenditures are included. There remains substantial unmet demand for treatment. The levels of expenditure on interdiction and source-country control are justified by neither historical experience nor economic analysis. And in study after study, prevention programs as implemented have consistently failed to reduce drug use among their subjects.

In sum, American drug policy deserves low marks. Yet simply assigning a bad grade does not make for constructive criticism. So in this final chapter, we take stock of what we think has been learned about the nature of the drug problem and the effects of drug-control programs and offer a short blueprint for improving the performance of American drug policy.

Domestic Enforcement

Suppression of domestic distribution has been the centerpiece of U.S. drug-control efforts. Intense enforcement has been justified on the grounds that it limits drug abuse by restricting the availability and raising the price of illicit drugs. There is little doubt that enforcement reduces drug use. Drugs are far more expensive (and difficult and risky to buy) than they would be in the absence of enforcement; price markups in drug markets are much greater than they are in both analogous legal markets and nominally illegal markets that face minimal enforcement, such as street markets for knockoff designer watches. And drug use is sensitive to price.

But enforcement faces diminishing marginal returns, and it is hard to find evidence that the sharp ratcheting-up of dealer risks since the late 1980s has done much to reduce availability or increase price. At the same time, however, there has been some good news about enforcement, which is that carefully crafted policing strategies can materially reduce drug-related crime and violence and the blight of open drug markets.

Clearly, retail-level drug enforcement should focus on what it can accomplish (reducing the negative side effects of illicit markets) and not on what it can't achieve (substantially raising drug prices). Thus, instead of aiming to arrest dealers and seize drugs—the mechanisms by which enforcement seeks to raise prices—retail drug enforcement should target individual dealers and organizations that engage in flagrant dealing, violence, and the recruitment of juveniles. Arrests and seizures should not be operational goals, but rather tools employed, with restraint, in the service of public safety.

Sentencing. Given limited prison capacity, it makes sense to give priority to housing the most active and violent offenders. Current sentencing policies fail to do this. Recent work by Sevigny and Caulkins (2004) shows that the vast majority of those incarcerated for drug offenses say that they were involved in distribution of some sort, even if convicted only of a possession offense. Nonetheless, only one-quarter of state drug inmates have a prior conviction for a violent crime, while nearly half have no prior nondrug conviction and were involved only in a minor role in their current offense. Long sentences for minor, nonviolent drug offenders are perhaps the least defensible aspect of current drug policy. Such sentences are wasteful of scarce prison space, have especially disparate racial impacts, and are particularly traumatic for the families of the incarcerated.

Sentencing laws and guidelines should be reformed to reduce total drug incarceration and to concentrate long sentences on those who engage in violence or recruit juveniles into the drug trade. Sentencing reform is especially important at the federal level, where prison terms are often determined more by the weight of the drugs involved than the conduct of the offender.

A perennially contentious issue in sentencing policy is how much discretion should be given to judges. In principle, discretion allows judges to tailor sentences to individual circumstances with much greater subtlety than a formula can, but judges are a diverse group, which means that discretion can also make sentencing more arbitrary. (Another consideration is that rigid sentencing formulas, such as mandatory minimums, effectively increase the power of prosecutorial discretion, which can also be used well or badly.) To our minds, a good sentencing formula will tend to be preferable to judicial discretion, and judicial discretion preferable to a bad sentencing formula. At the moment, there is enough bad sentencing law that increased judicial discretion would probably be an improvement in most jurisdictions.

Enforcement and the Epidemic Cycle. Most drug-related harm arises from the lasting effects of occasional drug epidemics. There are no plausible strategies for systematically preventing the occurrence of an epidemic; it is impossible to predict which drugs are likely to become popular, where the epidemic will start, or who will be the pioneers. It may sometimes be possible, however, to reduce the severity of an epidemic by slowing the speed with which it unfolds.

It therefore seems useful to try to shift enforcement efforts from drugs with large established markets to ones whose markets are small and potentially growing. This makes the most sense with enforcement that is more focused on distribution networks than street markets. With new drugs, high-level enforcement may be able to slow the development of a distribution infrastructure; with established drugs, that infrastructure already exists and is highly resilient.

This all sounds straightforward, but it is not. Shutting down distribution networks requires a level of intelligence that is difficult to muster before a drug has developed stable distribution networks. As Jonathan Caulkins has suggested, the early stages of a drug's distribution involve social rather than commercial networks; these are difficult to penetrate, particularly when the early users have little contact with the criminal justice system (Caulkins 2000). And because it is difficult to make cases in new markets, they can be relatively unattractive targets for enforcement agents and agencies. Nonetheless, it's hard to see why enforcement policy shouldn't make emerging drug threats a higher priority.

Source-Country Control. Economic reasoning argues against crop eradication and alternative development as supply-reduction strategies. But there are two historical cases in which crop eradication demonstrated a capacity to reduce U.S. drug consumption materially: the Turkish opium ban in the early 1970s and the spraying of Mexican poppy fields later in the decade. In both situations, however, the relevant source country was the largest supplier to the U.S. market; the reductions in drug cultivation were massive, at least 50 percent; the control programs were sudden, almost out-of-the-blue steps, rather than an escalation of existing crop-control efforts; the authority of the governments was basically unchallenged in the growing areas; and revenues from drug production and trafficking were, by the standards of most drug-exporting countries, a small part of national and regional economies.

The lesson we draw from this history is that crop eradication can make sense in those rare cases when such conditions are present, but it should not otherwise be a routine part of international drug-control efforts. Ordinary crop eradication has little chance of creating major and unanticipated shortages in supply, and because it prompts farmers to increase cultivation (perhaps exacerbating environmental damage) and hide their plants, it makes future eradication that much more difficult. To boot, eradication programs often run counter to American foreign policy objectives—when central governments are weak or unpopular in growing areas, or when drug revenues are a major contributor to the regional or national economy, eradication is likely to undermine government authority and support.

Interdiction. Economic reasoning and experience also raise doubts about the wisdom of a large commitment to interdiction. Despite considerable expenditures and some assistance from the military, import prices still account for only a small fraction of retail prices (roughly 10 percent in the case of cocaine), which suggests that interdiction does not impose a heavy cost on consumption. In cost-effectiveness and cost-benefit modeling, RAND found that an additional dollar spent on interdiction returned less than a dollar spent on domestic enforcement (Rydell and Everingham 1994).

Still, the economics of drug markets are not fully understood. Meanwhile, the volume of seizures is far from trivial, and seizures can provide enforcement agencies with avenues into trafficking organizations. It would therefore be rash to reduce interdiction spending sharply. A more prudential approach would be to enact modest cutbacks (say, 5 percent per year), remove the military from the business, and observe what happens.

Marijuana Enforcement. Marijuana is by far the most widely used illicit drug. It's also the most readily available and cheapest—a marijuana habit costs much less to support than a cocaine or heroin habit. Plainly, marijuana enforcement has a limited deterrent effect. Yet precisely because the drug is so widely and casually used, marijuana enforcement is particularly intrusive, nabbing many more non–problem users than cocaine or heroin enforcement. Much marijuana enforcement is simply unjustifiable—it does little to prevent problem use, but imposes great costs on non–problem users.

We believe that the case for imposing criminal sanctions for possession of small amounts of marijuana is weak. At least a dozen states have decriminalized marijuana possession to some degree,[2] and analysis of their experience suggests very modest effects on marijuana use, though recent research by Rosalie Pacula and colleagues has thrown doubt on the strength of the findings and suggested that decriminalization may increase by 2–3 percentage points the probability that an adolescent uses marijuana (Pacula, Chriqui, and King 2003; Hall and Pacula 2003). (Note that "decriminalization," as the term is customarily used in discussions of drug policy, implies the retention of civil penalties. Marijuana possession is still against the law in all states where it is decriminalized.) The arrest of 700,000 users each year should require a careful justification, given the minor harms of most marijuana use. Criminal convictions, even without serious penal sanctions, can cause great harm, as when an immigrant is deported solely on that basis. The much higher arrest rates for black as opposed to white users in recent years increases the urgency of the case for decriminalization.

There is also a reasonable argument for shrinking the black market for marijuana by allowing users to grow their own, an approach that has been adopted in a number of Australian jurisdictions. (For more details, see MacCoun and Reuter 2001, 356–64.) Moreover, like many other observers, we believe that although there is no empirical evidence one way or the other, drug prevention programs aimed at adolescents might be more effective following decriminalization. These programs could make a clearer distinction between marijuana and other drugs in terms of their dangers and thus increase the credibility of their messages about more dangerous substances.

Demand-Side Programs

Prevention. Everyone likes the idea of preventing kids from starting drug use or at least from going beyond experimentation. But there is no reason to believe we know how to immunize a large fraction of kids against drug abuse. A few experimental programs show promising results in reducing initiation, but it is unclear how they will perform when scaled up and put in the hands of schools, which for good reason are already under pressure to spend more of their limited class time on basic academic subjects. Until there is convincing evidence of cost-effectiveness, drug policy should not push school-based prevention programs.

Mass-media campaigns are notoriously difficult to evaluate because they are so diffuse; it is hard to find a control group so that one can distinguish the effects of the campaign from other factors affecting drug use. As already noted, the available evidence on the high-profile media campaign funded by the federal government in the past few years suggests that it has had no effect. Mass-media campaigns have shown success against tobacco in recent years. There are differences between the approaches of the two campaigns, and we conjecture that it is possible to learn from the successes of antitobacco campaigns what might make a difference for illicit drugs; but we lack the expertise to make specific recommendations.

Treatment. The case for expanding treatment is strong. Methadone and other pharmacological treatments (buprenorphine, naltrexone, and LAAM) for opioid dependence unquestionably help many heroin addicts cut down on their use of expensive illegal drugs, which has a direct effect on crime rates and HIV transmission. In addition to more money, opiate maintenance therapy needs fewer regulations. Treatment should be integrated into the health care system by allowing the provision of opioid medications in physicians' offices, as is being done on a trial basis with buprenorphine. Other mainstream treatments seem to make a difference, too. The ratios of benefits to costs, even when discounted to allow for the biases of the evaluators, are probably high.

But it's tough to get most addicts to enter treatment in the first place, and just as difficult to get them to stay. Building higher-quality drug treatment programs—programs not marginalized by the health care system— would no doubt help. Also promising is the enhanced use of enforcement as a recruiting scheme for treatment. Importantly, research shows that those coerced into treatment programs fare as well as those who volunteer. That being the case, the criminal justice system should make greater use of its authority to compel treatment for drug-involved offenders.

Targeting Heavy Users

No more than about 3.5 million Americans have substantial problems with cocaine and/or heroin. Not only do these 3.5 million account for the vast majority of cocaine and heroin consumption, they are probably responsible for an even larger share of the crime associated with drugs. Finding methods for reducing drug use in this population thus has very high payoffs. Increased treatment access and improved treatment quality can help accomplish this. There are, unfortunately, substantial limits to these interventions. It is hard to induce a large share of frequent users to enter treatment and similarly difficult to keep them in programs over a long period of time.

Since the late 1980s, Mark Kleiman has advocated taking advantage of the fact that at any one time a large share of the cocaine and heroin users causing greatest harm are under the supervision of the criminal justice system—on probation, parole, or pretrial release (Kleiman 1997). Kleiman (2001) suggests that frequent testing, accompanied by swift and modest but graduated sanctions for violations, could substantially reduce the number of active cocaine and heroin addicts. The political and bureaucratic obstacles to this intervention, which Kleiman has called "coerced abstinence," are considerable, but no other idea on the drawing board has the potential to reduce greatly the extent of drug abuse, drug-related crime, and imprisonment. If drug policymakers thought more like venture capitalists, they would make coerced abstinence a top priority.

Drug courts, an important innovation, could also take advantage of the observation that so many of the most problematic drug users are in the criminal justice system at any one time. There has been a veritable burgeoning of these courts, but even the roughly 1,200 that existed in 2002 still covered only about 1 percent of all criminal defendants. This is, to a significant degree, a consequence of the numerous restrictions on offender eligibility. In particular, the general restriction to those with nonviolent records means that these courts exclude a large share of frequent cocaine and heroin users. Thus drug courts may be a promising innovation in crime control, but it is less clear that they offer much for reductions in drug problems unless the conditions for acceptance into the programs are made much less restrictive.

Harm Reduction

No one professes opposition to the reduction of harm. Yet "harm reduction" is a highly controversial approach to drug-control policy. The paradox has arisen because harm reduction means different things to different people. MacCoun (1998b) has usefully drawn a distinction between micro– and macro–harm reduction. Micro–harm reduction, in MacCoun's terminology, involves reducing the harm per unit of drug use. By contrast, macro–harm reduction is aimed at reducing aggregate harm, which can be thought of as average harm per use multiplied by total use.

It's fair to say that most harm reduction proponents are in the micro camp, which leads them to favor not just the canonical harm reduction programs of needle-exchange and opiate maintenance therapy, but also a general relaxation of restrictions on currently illicit drug use (Nadelmann et al. 1994). All of this makes sense from the micro–harm reduction perspective; prohibition and enforcement worsen conditions for active drug users, so softening drug-control policies will reduce harm per unit of use. The catch, of course, is that micro–harm reduction policies might result in greater use, and therefore might not be harm reducing from the macro–harm reduction viewpoint.

In our view, harm reduction ought to mean macro–harm reduction. But remember that harm per unit of use (the focus of micro–harm reduction) is a component of macro–harm reduction. So although micro–harm reduction is incomplete, it's wrong to dismiss automatically, as many harm reduction opponents seem to, any efforts at micro–harm reduction. In most evaluations, for example, needle exchange appears to reduce disease transmission without any offsetting increase in drug use. Moreover, since U.S. drug policy tends to focus excessively if not exclusively on reducing the prevalence of use, harm reduction can be seen as a useful corrective.

Shifting the Burden of Proof

We have offered a series of suggestions for reducing the damage that drug use and drug control inflict upon American society: fewer incarcerations, better and more treatment, elimination of criminal penalties for marijuana possession, and implementation of coerced abstinence for drug-involved offenders are the most prominent. For none of them can we offer strong empirical evidence of substantial effectiveness.

However, we think that placing the burden of proof on those who argue for such policy changes favors a status quo that demonstrably harms some groups substantially and has little moral or empirical foundation. Tough enforcement, the centerpiece of American drug policy in terms of rhetoric, budget, and substance, has little to show by way of success. If, instead of putting 450,000 drug sellers and users into local jails and state and federal prisons, the nation were to lock up only 225,000, a great many people (both inmates and their families) would suffer less. It is surely reasonable to ask that those who would maintain the status quo offer some basis for believing the additional expense and suffering are justified.

Notes

Chapter 1: Historical Development

1. Epstein 1977 provides an entertaining account of this episode.

2. Len Bias, a University of Maryland basketball star who had recently been drafted by the Boston Celtics, and Don Rogers, a standout defensive back for the Cleveland Browns, died of cocaine overdoses on June 19 and 27, respectively.

3. "Cell-year" is a unit for counting the amount of prison space committed by judges when sentencing the population of defendants. Thus, if a judge gives five convicted defendants average sentences of ten years, the total cell-years committed is fifty.

4. Certification refers to a statutory requirement that the president certify that other nations that produce or export drugs to the United States have assisted the United States in the fight against drugs.

5. Indeed, it is said that ONDCP director Barry McCaffrey single-handedly changed President Clinton's mind on needle exchange. U.S. Department of Health and Human Services Secretary Donna Shalala had to cancel her announcement of federal financial support for needle exchange on the morning it was scheduled.

6. In 1998, Mayor Rudy Giuliani announced that New York City would end methadone maintenance for heroin addicts, pushing them into treatment programs that aimed at abstinence. Since the vast majority of methadone programs were funded by the state, not the city, this position was mostly rhetorical, and arguably allowed him to reap the political advantages of that position without suffering the adverse consequences of rising crime rates that widespread adoption of that policy might have created. The mayor later reversed his position.

Chapter 2: America's Drug Problems

1. Alcohol use rates also fluctuated, but at the aggregate level there was no strong relationship between rates of use of alcohol and illicit drugs.

2. The National Household Survey on Drug Abuse was conducted only once every two or three years prior to 1991, when it became an annual survey; hence the gaps in the data.

3. The survey changed its name from the somewhat threatening National Household Survey on Drug Abuse to the more neutral National Household Survey on Drug Use and Health, and respondents were provided incentive payments for participation. The result was an increase in response rates and in the percentages reporting drug use. It has proved impossible to disentangle these methodological effects from any real changes in drug use.

4. Official estimates of drug use omit the incarcerated, on the assumption that they do not continue to use drugs while in prison. The prevalence of drug use in prisons has been found to be relatively low (see U.S. Department of Justice, Bureau of Justice Statistics 1992), and those who do use probably consume small amounts per annum because they have access to few funds. Nonetheless, since most addicts who are incarcerated return to frequent drug use upon release, it is reasonable to include them in measures of the severity of the problem if one defines it as the number of persons whose lives are adversely affected by drug consumption.

5. In early 2004 the Department of Justice ended the ADAM program, which is a major loss for the monitoring of drug problems.

6. It is not true of cigarettes, since few users are able to maintain light use levels.

7. The 2003 MTF showed a sharp decline in prevalence for high school seniors from 9.2 percent in 2001 to 4.5 percent in 2003.

8. According to monthly data memoranda from the District of Columbia Pretrial Services Agency.

9. In 1994 Las Vegas, Los Angeles, Phoenix, San Diego, and San Francisco accounted for 424 of the 508 recorded deaths attributed to methamphetamine or speed in twenty-six metropolitan areas reporting to the medical examiner panel of the Drug Abuse Warning Network (U.S. Department of Health and Human Services, Substance Abuse and Mental Health Services Administration 1997).

10. The DAWN data are not entirely consistent with this. From 1995 to 2002, virtually all of the increase in cocaine and heroin mentions was in the "unexpected reaction" category. In fact, episodes for "chronic effects" were fewer in 2002 than in 1995 for both heroin and cocaine. Of course, "unexpected reactions" may be more likely as health deteriorates, and the category may serve as a catch-all for emergency visits and deaths brought on by causes other than overdoses.

11. Compton et al. (2004) report that the fraction of marijuana users who are abusing or dependent increased between 1991 and 2001. However, the abuse figure may be driven by the fact that one component for abuse under DSM-IV criteria is legal problems related to marijuana use; as discussed below, the fraction of marijuana users arrested has roughly doubled in the period 1991–2001. (DSM-IV refers to the fourth edition of the American Psychiatric Association's criteria for diagnosing mental disorders, which are published as *Diagnostic and Statistical Manual of Mental Disorders*.)

12. According to Ebener et al. (1993, A19), 60 percent of NHSDA respondents with a history of drug use report they are no longer using within five years of initiation. Most of these do not receive treatment.

13. The Monitoring the Future survey includes a question about whether the respondent has ever used marijuana daily or near-daily for at least one month. In 2003, while 16.4 percent of high school seniors reported having been daily or near-daily users at some point, only 6 percent reported current use on a daily or near-daily basis (U.S. Department of Health and Human Services, National Institute on Drug Abuse 2003, 380).

14. There is no good measure for this rate, given that the broad population surveys miss so many of those with problems of drug dependence. However, the household survey estimates that roughly 70 million persons have tried an illicit drug. A generous estimate of all those who have been dependent on cocaine, heroin, and marijuana in the last twenty-five years is 20 million. These are very crude figures.

15. This was famously captured in Tom Lehrer's song, *The Old Dope Peddler*:
> He gives the kids free samples
> Because he knows full well
> That today's young innocent faces
> Will be tomorrow's clientele.

16. There have been some increases in the number of younger users admitted for treatment and in the number of overdose deaths involving heroin among eighteen- to thirty-four-year-olds. On the other hand, the share of eighteen- to twenty-four-year-old arrestees testing positive for opiates has remained low. It is possible that there has been a modest epidemic among young, middle-class adults.

17. The consumption increase also reflected a decline in price that probably led to an increase in annual consumption per dependent user.

18. Hepatitis C is a long-latency infection that can easily be acquired from even a single use of a dirty needle.

19. Even with a 1.5 percent mortality rate and a generous estimate of 4 million frequent users, the mortality total is still substantially less than for alcohol, due to alcohol's much larger user base.

20. We ignore an anomalous 6.2 percent for Barcelona.

21. Assume, for the sake of argument, that of the $18 billion in estimated premature-death costs, $9 billion is attributable to drug abuse and $9 billion to policy, but that in the absence of that policy, there would be $20 billion in premature-death costs, all due to drug abuse. What, then, is the right figure for premature-death costs attributable to policy?

22. The estimates for 1992 from the same research group showed $148 billion for alcohol and $98 billion for illicit drugs (U.S. Department of Health and Human Services, National Institute on Drug Abuse 1998). The alcohol figure may have declined since then.

Chapter 3: Current Policies

1. The House Budget Committee makes initial allocations across the subcommittees but cannot transfer resources at the lower level.

2. See U.S. Office of National Drug Control Policy 1997, 84. No explicit justification was offered for this surprising classification. Presumably the argument was that community-oriented policing is more concerned with "preventing" crime problems (cf. Moore 1992) than with apprehending criminals; hence this kind of policing, inasmuch as it bears on drugs, is "preventative."

3. The minimum sentences for drug offenders have been raised in a series of acts since the Sentencing Reform Act of 1984, 18 U.S.C. §§ 3551 et seq. and 28 U.S.C. §§ 991–998, as amended.

4. Bennett equated consumption with demand, a practice that is common in the drug policy field but which misses the central point of the distinction between demand and supply. Decreases in consumption resulting from higher prices (rather than a reduced desire for drugs) might raise the earnings of drug sellers if demand is inelastic, and generally worsen various aspects of the drug problem. A reduction in demand with an unchanging supply curve lowers consumption without generating these undesirable side effects.

5. A world of true nonenforcement, as with knockoff designer watches sold on the streets of New York, might yield much higher availability. We are considering here shifts within the established regime of enforcement.

6. "Sell-and-bust" programs involve police officers masquerading as drug sellers. Other officers then arrest the customers. These tactics are discussed analytically in Kleiman 1997, 145.

7. Recent data from the Substance Abuse and Mental Health Services Administration's Treatment Episode Data Set (TEDS) show that less than 5 percent of women in treatment at any one time are pregnant. See U.S. Department of Health and Human Services, Substance Abuse and Mental Health Services Administration 2004b.

8. See, for example, Grinspoon and Bakalar 1994.

9. Most local prevention expenditures are probably made by school districts. Prevention expenditures are extremely difficult to estimate because schools do not split up their budgets on the basis of curriculum content. One crude but appealing method is to estimate what share of class time goes to drug prevention and then allocate to prevention the same share of the total budget for elementary and secondary education. That still leaves two problems: estimating class time devoted to prevention, and estimating the cost of nonschool prevention. It is likely that no more than 1 percent of school time goes to drug prevention, even broadly defined; that would suggest a 1991 expenditure total of less than $2.5 billion. (See U.S. Department of Education, National Center for Education Statistics 2003.) It is even less clear that independent hospital authorities and similar entities account for a significant share of total treatment expenditures.

10. The $3.2 billion estimate comes from U.S. Office of National Drug Control Policy 1993.

11. The Taliban did cut production of opium drastically in late 2000. The United Nations estimates that total production in 2001 (through the harvest season) totaled only 185 metric tons, compared to 3,276 metric tons in the previous year. There is little suggestion that U.S. policies played any role in this cutback.

12. Given the flow of Ecstasy from the Netherlands to the United States and the perceived insouciance of Dutch officials, there was consideration of requiring the Netherlands to obtain certification in 2003.

13. Indeed, Mexican certification has been provided without the president's having invoked the "national-interest waiver," which can be applied when other political considerations collide with evidence that a nation has not been cooperating with drug-control efforts.

14. One particularly troubling mode of smuggling is "body-packing," in which the smuggler swallows a number of packages of the drug wrapped in condoms or similar protective material. Enough body-packers have suffered drug overdoses when packages leaked or burst to have generated a small medical literature on the phenomenon. Not surprisingly, an early contribution to that literature came from an emergency room near the Los Angeles International Airport. The recent film *Maria Full of Grace* provides a poignant portrayal of that trade and its injuries.

15. Given the pyramid-like nature of the distribution system, where a 250-kilogram international shipment is divided up through several stages of wholesale and retail dealing, and eventually sold at retail in as many as 250,000 one-gram transactions, perhaps fewer than 1 percent of all those involved in the drug trade can be considered high-level principals.

16. No treatment gap was estimated for 1999.

17. The excessive use of hospital-based treatment modalities can be explained by the rapid growth of private insurance coverage during the 1980s. State-mandated benefits tended to be more generous for inpatient than outpatient care, and many insurers favored hospital-based care because it resembled other forms of medical treatment. Thus, by 1989, 60 percent of all private insurance payments for drug treatment went to hospital-based care. See Schlesinger and Dorwart 1992, 205.

18. CREW 2000's website is at http://www.drug-prevention.de/edin_crew2000/crew_eng/index_doc.htm.

Chapter 4: Policy Effectiveness

1. Anti-Drug Abuse Act of 1988, 21 U.S.C. §1705(b)(1)(E)(2).

2. At the street level, heroin is typically sold in $10 units, commonly referred to as "dime bags."

3. The estimate is constructed from a set of reasonable assumptions but has never been tested with actual data.

4. For a contrary argument, see Miron 2003.

5. A recent study examined thirty-nine drug-trafficking organizations prosecuted in federal courts in New York City between 1984 and 1997. Only six were deemed to be "corporations," organizations with "a formal hierarchy and a well-defined division of labor." See Natarajan and Belanger 1998.

6. For example, the arrests bring new dealers into the market and may break up existing territorial agreements. New dealers also have less basis for trust in transactions with wholesalers and may be more likely to resort to violence as a consequence. This is highly conjectural; as with almost all interesting propositions about drug markets, there are no data available for testing it.

7. The federal legislation creating TANF (the Personal Responsibility and Work Opportunity Reconciliation Act of 1996) does not specify how the states should deal with substance abuse among clients; the primary incentive for the states to confront the problem comes from the need to achieve high employment rates among welfare clients within specified time periods. The statute does allow for testing without requiring prior federal approval.

8. Data were drawn from the Treatment Outcome Prospective Study (TOPS), the largest longitudinal study of drug treatment in the 1980s.

9. Jonathan Caulkins has pointed out that all of these estimates would be considerably higher if the study were redone today. RAND researchers believe that the per-kilogram social costs of cocaine use are about triple those assumed for the *Controlling Cocaine* study, and that cocaine use is about twice as responsive to prices as previously thought.

10. By way of disclosure, both authors have been involved in this issue. Reuter was director of the RAND Drug Policy Research Center at the time the study was being done and was also a reviewer of an early draft. Boyum was paid by RAND to review its response to the NRC assessment of the RAND study.

Chapter 5: Policy Reform

1. It is striking that none of the big longitudinal health studies that investigate cancer has included questions about marijuana use, despite the evidence that the drug is rich in carcinogens and has been widely used over the last thirty years. Conversations with epidemiologists suggest a general concern about response rates and perhaps even a political correctness in a generally liberal research community.

2. The states commonly viewed as decriminalized are Alaska, Arizona, California, Colorado, Maine, Minnesota, Mississippi, Nebraska, New York, North

Carolina, Ohio, and Oregon. However, Pacula, Chriqui, and King (2003) point out that this list is somewhat arbitrary. While Alaska, Arizona, California, and North Carolina have eliminated jail time as a penalty, they still specify possession as a criminal offense. And seven other states (Connecticut, Louisiana, Massachusetts, New Jersey, Vermont, West Virginia, and Wisconsin) specify first-time marijuana possession as a noncriminal offense.

References

American Psychiatric Association. 1994. *Diagnostic and Statistical Manual of Mental Disorders DSM-IV.* 4th edition. Washington, D.C.: American Psychiatric Association.

Anglin, M. Douglas, and Yih-Ing Hser. 1990. Treatment of Drug Abuse. In *Drugs and Crime*, ed. Michael H. Tonry and James Q. Wilson, 393–460. Vol. 13 of *Crime and Justice: A Review of Research.* Chicago: University of Chicago Press.

Ball, John C., Lawrence Rosen, John A. Flueck, and David N. Nurco. 1981. The Criminality of Heroin Addicts: When Addicted and when Off Opiates. In *The Drugs-Crime Connection*, ed. James A. Inciardi, 39–65. Beverly Hills, Calif.: Sage Publications.

Botvin, Gilbert J., and Elizabeth Botvin. 1997. School-Based Programs. In *Substance Abuse: A Comprehensive Textbook*, ed. Joyce H. Lowinson, Pedro Ruiz, Robert B. Millman, and John G. Langrod, 764–75. 3rd ed. Philadelphia: Williams & Wilkins.

Bourgois, Phillipe. 1996. *In Search of Respect: Selling Crack in El Barrio.* New York: Cambridge University Press.

Boyum, David. 1992. Reflections on Economic Theory and Drug Enforcement. PhD dissertation, Harvard University.

————. 1993. *Heroin and Cocaine Market Structure.* Prepared for the Office of National Drug Control Policy. Cambridge, Mass.: BOTEC Analysis Corporation.

Brownsberger, William N. 1997. Prevalence of Frequent Cocaine Use in Urban Poverty Areas. *Contemporary Drug Problems* 24 (2): 349–71.

Bushway, Shawn, Jonathan P. Caulkins, and Peter Reuter. 2003. Does State and Local Drug Enforcement Raise Drug Prices? Unpublished paper, University of Maryland.

Callahan, J. J., D. S. Shepard, R. H. Beinecke, M. Larson, and D. Cavanaugh. 1995. Mental Health/Substance Abuse Treatment in Managed Care: The Massachusetts Medicaid Experience. *Health Affairs* 14 (3): 173–84.

Carnevale, J. T., and P. J. Murphy. 1999. Matching Rhetoric to Dollars: Twenty-five Years of Federal Drug Strategies and Drug Budgets. *Journal of Drug Issues* 29 (2): 299–322.

Caulkins, Jonathan P. 1990. The Distribution and Consumption of Illicit Drugs: Some Mathematical Models and Their Policy Implications. PhD dissertation, Massachusetts Institute of Technology.

————. 1998. The Cost-Effectiveness of Civil Remedies: The Case of Drug Control Interventions. In *Civil Remedies and Crime Prevention*, ed. Lorraine Green Mazerolle and Janice Roehl. Crime Prevention Studies 9:219–37. Monsey, N.Y.: Criminal Justice Press.

————. 2000. The Evolution of Drug Initiation: From Social Networks to Public Markets. In *Optimization, Dynamics, and Economic Analysis*, ed. E. J. Dockner, R. F. Hartl, M. Luptacik, and G. Sorger, 353–67. Heidelberg: Physica-Verlag.

————. 2001. The Dynamic Character of Drug Problems. *Bulletin on Narcotics* 53 (1): 11–23.

Caulkins, Jonathan P., and P. Ebener. 1995. Describing DAWN's Dominion. *Contemporary Drug Problems* 22 (3): 547–67.

Caulkins, Jonathan P., and Peter Reuter. 1997. Setting Goals for Drug Policy: Harm Reduction or Use Reduction? *Addiction* 97 (9): 1143–50.

————. 1998. What Can We Learn from Drug Prices? *Journal of Drug Issues* 28 (3): 593–612.

Caulkins, Jonathan P., C. Peter Rydell, Susan S. Everingham, James R. Chiesa, and Shawn Bushway. 1999. *An Ounce of Prevention, a Pound of Uncertainty: The Cost-Effectiveness of School-Based Drug Prevention Programs*. Santa Monica, Calif.: RAND.

Center on Addiction and Substance Abuse. 1994. *Cigarette, Alcohol, Marijuana: Gateways to Illicit Drug Use*. New York: Columbia University.

Chaffin, Mark J., Kelly J. Kelleher, and Janice A. Hollenberg. 1996. Onset of Physical Abuse and Neglect: Psychiatric, Substance Abuse, and Social Risk Factors from Prospective Community Data. *Child Abuse and Neglect* 20 (3): 191–203.

Compton, Wilson M., Bridget F. Grant, James D. Colliver, Meyer D. Glantz, and Frederick S. Stinson. 2004. Prevalence of Marijuana Use Disorders in the United States: 1991–1992 and 2001–2002. *JAMA* 291:2114–21.

Cork, Daniel. 1999. Examining Space–Time Interaction in City-Level Homicide Data: Crack Markets and the Diffusion of Guns among Youth. *Journal of Quantitative Criminology* 15 (4): 379–406.

Cornish, J. W., D. Metzger, G. E. Woody, D. Wilson, A. T. McLellan, B. Vandergrift, and C. P. O'Brien. 1997. Naltrexone Pharmacotherapy for Opioid Dependent Federal Probationers. *Journal of Substance Abuse Treatment* 14 (6): 529–34.

Courtwright, David T. 1995. The Rise and Fall and Rise of Cocaine in the United States. In *Consuming Habits: Drugs in History and Anthropology*, ed. J. Goodman, P. E. Lovejoy, and A. Sherratt. London: Routledge.

Des Jarlais, Don C., Samuel R. Friedman, Jo L. Sotheran, John Wenston, Michael Marmor, Stanley R. Yancovitz, Blanche Frank, Sara Beatrice, and Donna Mildvan. 1994. Continuity and Change within an HIV Epidemic: Injecting Drug Users in New York City, 1984 through 1992. *JAMA* 271 (2): 121–27.

Des Jarlais, Don C., Theresa Perlis, Samuel R. Friedman, Sherry Deren, Timothy Chapman, Jo L. Sotheran, Stephanie Tortu, Mark Beardsley, Denise Paone,

Lucia V. Torian, Sara T. Beatrice, Erica DeBernardo, Edgar Monterroso, and Michael Marmor. 1998. Declining Seroprevalence in a Very Large HIV Epidemic: Injecting Drug Users in New York City, 1991 to 1996. *American Journal of Public Health* 88 (12): 1801–6.

Des Jarlais, Don C., and Anne Schuchat. 2001. Hepatitis C among Drug Users: Déjà Vu All Over Again? *American Journal of Public Health* 91 (1): 21–22.

Drug Strategies. 1996. *Making the Grade: A Guide to School Drug Prevention Programs*. Washington, D.C.: Drug Strategies.

Ebener, Patricia A., Jonathan P. Caulkins, Sandy A. Geschwind, Daniel L. McCaffrey, and Hilary L. Saner. 1993. *Improving Data and Analysis to Support National Substance Abuse Policy*. Santa Monica, Calif.: RAND.

Eddy, Mark. 2003. *War on Drugs: The National Youth Anti-Drug Media Campaign*. Washington, D.C.: Congressional Research Service.

Ellickson, P. L., R. D. Hays, and R. M. Bell. 1992. Stepping through the Drug Use Sequence: Longitudinal Scalogram Analysis of Initiation and Regular Use. *Journal of Abnormal Psychology* 101 (3): 441–51.

Epstein, Edward J. 1977. *Agency of Fear*. New York: Putnam.

European Monitoring Centre for Drugs and Drug Addiction. 2002. *2002 Annual Report on the State of the Drugs Problem in the European Union and Norway*. Luxembourg: Office for Official Publications of the European Communities.

Faggiano, F., F. Vigna-Taglianti, E. Versino, and P. Lemma. 2004. Methadone Maintenance at Different Dosages for Opioid Dependence (Cochrane Review). In *The Cochrane Library*, Issue 3, 2004. Chichester, UK: John Wiley & Sons, Ltd.

Farrelly, M. C., D. M. Fergusson, and L. J. Horwood. 2003. Youth Tobacco Prevention Mass Media Campaigns: Past, Present, and Future Directions. *Tobacco Control* 12 (2): 35–47.

Fergusson, D. M., and L. J. Horwood. 1997. Early Onset Cannabis Use and Psychosocial Adjustment in Young Adults. *Addiction* 92 (2): 279–96.

———. 2000. Does Cannabis Use Encourage Other Forms of Illicit Drug Use? *Addiction* 95 (4): 505–20.

Fiellin, David A., Patrick G. O'Connor, Marek Chawarski, Juliana P. Pakes, Michael V. Pantalon, and Richard S. Schottenfeld. 2001. Methadone Maintenance in Primary Care: A Randomized Controlled Trial. *JAMA* 286 (14): 1724–31.

Fuentes, Joseph R. 1998. *Life of a Cell: Managerial Practice and Strategy in Colombian Cocaine Distribution in the United States*. PhD dissertation, City University of New York.

Godshaw, G., R. Koppell, and R. Pancoast. 1987. *Anti-Drug Law Enforcement Efforts and Their Impact*. Bala Cynwyd, Pa.: Wharton Econometric Forecasting Associates.

Goldberg, Peter. 1980. The Federal Government's Response to Illicit Drugs, 1969–1978. In *The Facts about "Drug Abuse,"* by the Drug Abuse Council. New York: The Free Press.

Goldstein, Paul J., Henry H. Brownstein, Patrick J. Ryan, and Patricia A. Bellucci. 1989. Crack and Homicide in New York City, 1988: A Conceptually-Based Event Analysis. *Contemporary Drug Problems* 16 (Winter): 651–87

Golub, Andrew, and Bruce Johnson. 2001. Variation in Youthful Risks of Progression from Alcohol and Tobacco to Marijuana and to Hard Drugs across Generations. *American Journal of Public Health* 91 (2): 225–32.

Gottfredson, G. D., D. C. Gottfredson, E. R. Czeh, D. Cantor, S. B. Crosse, and I. Hantman. 2000. *A National Study of Delinquency Prevention in School: Final Report.* ERIC No. ED 459 409. Ellicott City, Md.: Gottfredson Associates Inc. http://www.gottfredson.com.

Gottfredson, Denise, David Wilson, and Stacy Skroban Najaka. 2002. School-Based Crime Prevention. In *Evidence-Based Crime Prevention*, ed. Lawrence W. Sherman, David P. Farrington, Doris Layton MacKenzie, and Brandon C. Welsh, 56–164. London: Routledge.

Grinspoon, Lester, and James Bakalar. 1994. The War on Drugs: A Peace Proposal. *New England Journal of Medicine* 330 (3): 357–60.

Hall, Wayne, and Rosalie Licardo Pacula. 2003. *Cannabis Use and Dependence: Public Health and Public Policy.* Cambridge: Cambridge University Press.

Harper, Tim. 2003. Pot Plan Puts U.S. Noses Out of Joint. *Toronto Star*, May 3, 2003. A1.

Harrell, Adele, Shane Cavanagh, and John Roman. 1998. *Findings from the Evaluation of the D.C. Superior Court Intervention Program: Final Report.* Washington, D.C.: The Urban Institute.

Hodgkin, D., D. S. Shepard, Y. E. Anthony, and G. K. Strickler. 2004. A Publicly Managed Medicaid Substance Abuse Carve-Out: Effects on Spending and Utilization. *Administration and Policy in Mental Health* 31 (3): 197–217.

Hornik, Robert, David Maklan, Diane Cadell, Carlin Henry Barmada, Lela Jacobsohn, Amalia Prado, Anca Romantan, Robert Orwin, Sanjeev Sridharan, Elaine Zanutto, Robert Baskin, Adam Chu, Carol Morin, Kristie Taylor, and Diane Steele. 2002. Executive summary for *Evaluation of the National Youth Anti-Drug Media Campaign: Fifth Semi-Annual Report of Findings.* Rockville, Md.: Westat.

Hser, Yi-Ing, V. Hoffman, C. E. Grella, and M. Douglas Anglin. 2001. A 33-Year Follow-Up of Narcotics Addicts. *Archives of General Psychiatry* 58 (5): 503–8.

Hubbard, Robert. L., Mary Ellen Marsden, J. Valley Rachal, Hendrick J. Harwood, Elizabeth R. Cavanaugh, and Harold M. Ginsburg. 1989. *Drug Abuse Treatment: A National Study of Effectiveness.* Chapel Hill, N.C.: University of North Carolina Press.

Hunt, Leon G., and Carl D. Chambers. 1976. *The Heroin Epidemics: A Study of Heroin Use in the United States, 1965–1975.* New York: Spectrum Books.

Institute of Medicine. Committee for the Study of Treatment and Rehabilitation Services for Alcoholism and Alcohol Abuse. 1990. *Broadening the Base of Treatment for Alcohol Problems: Report of a Study by a Committee of the Institute of Medicine, Division of Mental Health and Behavioral Medicine.* Washington, D.C.: National Academy Press.

Jencks, Christopher. 1994. *The Homeless.* Cambridge, Mass.: Harvard University Press.

Johnson, Rolley E., Mary Ann Chutuape, Eric C. Strain, Sharon L. Walsh, Maxine L. Stitzer, and George E. Bigelow. 2000. A Comparison of Levomethadyl Acetate, Buprenorphine, and Methadone for Opioid Dependence. *New England Journal of Medicine* 343 (18): 1290–97.

Kaestner, Robert. 1991. The Effects of Illicit Drug Use on the Wages of Young Adults. *Journal of Labor Economics* 9 (4): 381–412.

Kandel, Denise B. 1993. The Social Demography of Drug Use. *The Milbank Quarterly* 69:365–414.

Kennedy, Randall. 1997. *Race, Crime, and the Law.* New York: Pantheon.

Kleiman, Mark A. R. 1992. *Against Excess: Drug Policy for Results.* New York: Basic Books.

———. 1997. Coerced Abstinence: A Neopaternalist Drug Policy Initiative. In *The New Paternalism: Supervisory Approaches to Poverty*, ed. Lawrence M. Mead, 182–219. Washington, D.C.: Brookings Institution.

———. 2001. Controlling Drug Use and Crime with Testing, Sanctions and Treatment. In *Drug Addiction and Drug Policy: The Struggle to Control Dependence*, ed. Philip Heymann and William Brownsberger, 168–92. Cambridge, Mass.: Harvard University Press.

Kozel, Nicholas J., and E. H. Adams. 1986. Epidemiology of Drug Abuse: An Overview. *Science* 234 (4779): 970–74.

Kuziemko, Ilyana, and Steven Levitt. 2004. An Empirical Analysis of Imprisoning Drug Offenders. *Journal of Public Economics* 88 (9–10): 2043–66.

Legal Action Center. 1997. *Making Welfare Reform Work: Tools for Confronting Alcohol and Drug Problems Among Recipients.* New York: Legal Action Center.

Leshner, Alan I. 1997. National Study Offers Strong Evidence of the Effectiveness of Drug Abuse Treatment. *NIDA Notes* 12 (5). http://www.drugabuse.gov/NIDA_Notes/NNVol12N5/DirRepVol12N5.html.

Lynskey, Michael T., Andrew C. Heath, Kathleen K. Bucholz, Wendy S. Slutske, Pamela A. F. Madden, Elliot C. Nelson, Dixie J. Statham, and Nicholas G. Martin. 2003. Escalation of Drug Use in Early-Onset Cannabis Users vs. Co-Twin Controls. *JAMA* 289 (4): 427–33.

MacCoun, Robert. 1998a. In What Sense (If Any) Is Marijuana a Gateway Drug? *Drug Policy Analysis Bulletin*, no. 4. http://www.fas.org/drugs/issue4.htm#gateway (accessed March 7, 2003).

———. 1998b. Biases in the Interpretation and Use of Research Results. *Annual Review of Psychology* 49:259–87.

MacCoun, Robert, and Peter Reuter. 2001. *Drug War Heresies: Learning from Other Vices, Times and Places.* New York: Cambridge University Press.

Manski, Charles F., John V. Pepper, and Carol Petrie. 2001. *Informing America's Policy on Illegal Drugs: What We Don't Know Keeps Hurting Us.* Washington, D.C.: National Academy Press.

Manski, Charles F., John V. Pepper, and Yonette F. Thomas, eds. 1999. *Assessment of Two Cost-Effectiveness Studies on Cocaine Control Policy.* Washington, D.C.: National Academy Press.

Massing, Michael. 1998. *The Fix.* New York: Simon & Schuster.

McGlothlin, William C., M. Douglas Anglin, and Bruce D. Wilson. 1977. *An Evaluation of the California Civil Addict Program.* Rockville, Md.: National Institute on Drug Abuse.

Miller, W. R., and R. K. Hester. 1986. Inpatient Alcohol Treatment: Who Benefits? *American Psychologist* 41:794–805.

Minow, Martha. 1997. Judge for the Situation: Judge Jack Weinstein, Creator of Temporary Administrative Agencies. *Columbia Law Review* 97:2010–33.

Miron, Jeffrey. 2003. The Effect of Drug Prohibition on Prices: Evidence from the Markets for Cocaine and Heroin. *Review of Economics and Statistics* 85 (3): 522–30.

Moore, Mark. 1973. Achieving Discrimination in the Effective Price of Heroin. *American Economic Review* 63 (2): 270–77.

———. 1992. Community Policing. In *Modern Policing*, ed. Michael Tonry and Norval Morris. Chicago: University of Chicago Press.

Morral, Andrew R., Dan F. McCaffrey, and Susan M. Paddock. 2002. Reassessing the Marijuana Gateway Effect. *Addiction* 97 (12): 1493–1504.

Mueller, Michael D, and June R. Wyman. 1997. Study Sheds New Light on the State of Drug Abuse Treatment Nationwide. *NIDA Notes* 12, no. 5. http://www.drugabuse.gov/NIDA_Notes/NNVol12N5/Study.html (accessed November 19, 2004).

Murphy, Patrick. 1994. *Keeping Score: The Frailties of the Federal Drug Control Budget.* Santa Monica, Calif.: RAND.

Murphy, Patrick, Lynn E. Davis, Timothy Liston, David Thaler, and Kathi Webb. 2000. *Improving Anti-Drug Budgeting.* Santa Monica, Calif.: RAND.

Musto, David F. 1999. *The American Disease.* 3rd ed. New York: Oxford University Press.

Nadelmann, Ethan, Peter Cohen, Ernest Drucker, Ueli Locher, Gerry Stimson, and Alex Wodak. 1994. The Harm Reduction Approach to Drug Policy: International Progress. Unpublished manuscript. New York: Lindesmith Center.

Natarajan, Mangai, and Mathieu Belanger. 1998. Varieties of Drug Trafficking Organizations: A Typology of Cases Prosecuted in New York City. *Journal of Drug Issues* 28 (4): 1005–26.

National Consensus Development Panel on Effective Medical Treatment of Opiate Addiction. 1998. Effective Medical Treatment of Opiate Addiction. *JAMA* 280 (22): 1936–43.

O'Connor, Patrick G., Alison H. Oliveto, Julia M. Shi, E. G. Triffleman, Kathleen M. Carroll, Thomas R. Kosten, Bruce J. Rounsaville, Juliana P. Pakes, and Richard S. Schottenfeld. 1998. A Randomized Trial of Buprenorphine Maintenance for Heroin Dependence in a Primary Care Clinic for Substance Users versus a Methadone Clinic. *American Journal of Medicine* 105 (2): 100–105.

Office of the Press Secretary. 2001. Remarks by President George W. Bush and President Vicente Fox of Mexico in Joint Press Conference, February 16, 2001. http://www.whitehouse.gov/news/releases/2001/02/print/20010216-3.html (accessed November 17, 2004).

Okuyemi, Kolawole S., Kari Jo Harris, Monica Scheibmeir, Won S. Choi, Joshua Powell, and Jasjit S. Ahluwalia. 2002. Light Smokers: Issues and Recommendations. *Nicotine & Tobacco Research* 4 (4, Supplement 2): 103–12.

Pacula, Rosalie Licardo, Jamie F. Chriqui, and Joanna King. 2003. Marijuana Decriminalization: What Does It Mean in the United States? Working paper 9690. Cambridge, Mass.: National Bureau of Economic Research.

Pew Research Center for the People and the Press. 2001. Interdiction and Incarceration Still Top Remedies. http://people-press.org/reports/print.php3?ReportID=16 (accessed March 9, 2003).

Pollack, Harold A. 2000. When Pregnant Women Use Crack. *Drug Policy Analysis Bulletin*, no. 8 (February). http://www.fas.org/drugs/issue8.htm (accessed April 16, 2003).

———. 2001a. The Cost-Effectiveness of Harm Reduction in Preventing Hepatitis C. *Medical Decision Making* 21 (5): 357–67.

———. 2001b. Ignoring "Downstream Infection" in the Evaluation of Harm Reduction Interventions for Injection Drug Users. *European Journal of Epidemiology* 17 (4): 391–95.

Pollack, H.A., S. Danziger, K.S. Seefeldt, and R. Jayakody. 2002. Substance Use among Welfare Recipients: Trends and Policy Responses. *Social Service Review* 76 (2): 256–74.

Register, C., and D. Williams. 1992. Labor Market Effects of Marijuana and Cocaine Use among Young Men. *Industrial and Labor Relations Review* 45 (3): 435–48.

Rettig, Richard A., and Adam Yarmolinsky, eds. 1995. *Federal Regulation of Methadone Treatment.* Committee on Federal Regulation of Methadone Treatment, Institute of Medicine. Washington, D.C.: National Academy Press.

Reuter, Peter. 1985. Eternal Hope: America's Quest for Narcotics Control. *The Public Interest* (Spring): 79–95.

———. 1995. The Decline of the American Mafia. *The Public Interest* (Summer): 89–99.

———. 1999. Are Calculations of the Economic Costs of Drug Abuse Either Possible or Useful? *Addiction* 94 (5): 627–30

———. 2001. Why Does Research Have So Little Impact on American Drug Policy? *Addiction* 96 (3): 373–76.

Reuter, Peter, Gordon Crawford, and Jonathan Cave. 1988. *Sealing the Borders: Effects of Increased Military Efforts in Drug Interdiction*, R-3594-USDP. Santa Monica, Calif.: RAND.

Reuter, Peter, and Victoria Greenfield. 2001. Measuring Global Drug Markets: How Good Are the Numbers and Why Should We Care about Them? *World Economics* 2 (4): 159–73.

Reuter, Peter, Paul Hirschfield, and Curt Davies. 2001. Assessing the Crack-Down on Marijuana in Maryland. www.abell.org/publications/detail.asp?ID=66 (accessed July 22, 2004).

Reuter, Peter, and Mark A. R. Kleiman. 1986. Risks and Prices. In *Crime and Justice, An Annual Review of Research*, ed. Michael Tonry and Norval Morris, 7:289–340. Chicago: University of Chicago Press.

Reuter, Peter, Robert MacCoun, and Patrick Murphy. 1990. *Money from Crime*. Santa Monica, Calif.: RAND.

Rose, Geoffrey. 1992. *The Strategy of Preventive Medicine*. Oxford: Oxford University Press.

Rubin, Robert E. 1999. Remarks to the University of Pennsylvania commencement. Philadelphia, May 17.

Rydell, C. Peter, and Susan S. Everingham. 1994. *Controlling Cocaine: Supply versus Demand Programs*. MR-331-ONDCP/A/DPRC. Santa Monica, Calif.: RAND.

Saner, Hilary, Robert MacCoun, and Peter Reuter. 1995. On the Ubiquity of Drug Selling among Youthful Offenders in Washington, D.C., 1985–1991: Age, Period, or Cohort Effect? *Journal of Quantitative Criminology* 11 (4): 337–62.

Satel, Sally. 2001. *PC, M.D.: How Political Correctness Is Corrupting Medicine*. New York: Basic Books.

Schlesinger, Mark, and Robert Dorwart. 1992. Falling between the Cracks: Failing National Strategies for the Treatment of Substance Abuse. *Dædalus* 121 (Summer): 205.

Schlosser, Eric. 1994. Reefer Madness. *The Atlantic Monthly* 274 (August): 45–58.

———. 1997. More Reefer Madness. *The Atlantic Monthly* 279 (April): 90–98.

Sees, Karen L., Kevin L. Delucchi, Carmen Masson, Amy Rosen, H. Westley Clark, Helen Robillard, Peter Banys, and Sharon M. Hall. 2000. Methadone Maintenance versus 180-Day Psychosocially-Enriched Detoxification for Treatment of Opioid Dependence: A Randomized, Controlled Trial. *JAMA* 283 (March 8): 1303–10.

Sevigny, Eric, and Jonathan Caulkins. 2004. Kingpins or Mules: An Analysis of Drug Offenders Incarcerated in Federal and State Prisons. *Criminology and Public Policy* 3 (3): 401–34.

Shedler, Jonathan, and Jack Block. 1990. Adolescent Drug Use and Psychological Health: A Longitudinal Inquiry. *American Psychologist* 45:612–30.

Spillane, Joseph F. 2000. *Cocaine: From Medical Marvel to Modern Menace in the United States, 1884–1920.* Baltimore, Md.: The Johns Hopkins University Press.

Strain, Eric. C., George E. Bigelow, Ira A. Liebson, and Maxine L. Stitzer. 1999. Moderate- vs High-Dose Methadone in the Treatment of Opioid Dependence: A Randomized Trial. *JAMA* 281 (11): 1000–1005.

Strumwasser, I., N. V. Paranjpe, M. Udow, D. Share, M. Wisgerhof, D. L. Ronis, C. Bartzack, and A. N. Saad. 1991. Appropriateness of Psychiatric and Substance Abuse Hospitalization: Implications for Payment and Utilization Management. *Medical Care* 29 (Supplement): AS77–AS90.

Thompson, J. W., B. J. Burns, H. H. Goldman, and J. Smith. 1992. Initial Level of Care and Clinical Status in a Managed Mental Health Program. *Hospital and Community Psychiatry* 43 (6): 599–603.

Tonry, Michael. 1995. *Malign Neglect.* New York: Oxford University Press.

United Nations Office for Drug Control and Crime Prevention. 2002. *Global Illicit Drug Trends 2002.* New York: United Nations.

United Nations Office on Drugs and Crime. 2003a. *Global Illicit Drug Trends 2003.* New York: United Nations.

———. 2003b. *The Opium Economy in Afghanistan: An International Problem.* New York: United Nations.

———. 2004. *2004 World Drug Report.* New York: United Nations.

U.S. Bureau of the Census. 1993. *State and Local Expenditures on Drug Control Activities.* Washington, D.C.: Government Printing Office.

U.S. Congress. Office of Technology Assessment. 1983. *The Effectiveness and Costs of Alcohol Treatment.* By Leonard Saxe, with Denise Dougherty, Katherine Esty, and Michelle Fine. Health Technology Case Study 22. Washington, D.C.: Government Printing Office.

U.S. Department of Education. National Center for Educational Statistics. 2003. *Digest of Education Statistics, 2002.* By Thomas D. Snyder. NCES 2003–060. Washington, D.C.: U.S. Department of Education.

U.S. Department of Health and Human Services. Centers for Disease Control and Prevention. 2003a. *HIV/AIDS Surveillance Report: Cases of HIV Infection and AIDS in the United States, 2002,* vol. 14. Atlanta, Ga.: U.S. Department of Health and Human Services, Centers for Disease Control.

———. 2003b. Deaths: Final Data for 2001. By Elizabeth Arias, Robert N. Anderson, Hsiang-Ching Kung, Sherry L. Murphy, and Kenneth D. Kochanek. *National Vital Statistics Reports* 52 (3). http://www.cdc.gov/nchs/data/nvsr/nvsr52/nvsr52_03.pdf (accessed August 17, 2004).

U.S. Department of Health and Human Services. National Institute on Drug Abuse. 1998. *The Economic Costs of Alcohol and Drug Abuse in the United States—1992.* By Henrick Harwood, Douglas Fountain, and Gina Livermore. Rockville, Md.: U.S. Department of Health and Human Services, National Institute on Drug Abuse.

————. 1999. *Principles of Drug Abuse Treatment: A Research-Based Guide*. NIH publication no. 00-4180. Rockville, Md.: U.S. Department of Health and Human Services, National Institute on Drug Abuse.

————. 2002. *Secondary School Students*. Vol. 1 of *Monitoring the Future National Survey Results on Drug Use, 1975–2001*. By Lloyd D. Johnston, Patrick M. O'Malley, and Jerald G. Bachman. NIH publication no. 02-5106. Bethesda, Md.: U.S. Department of Health and Human Services, National Institute on Drug Abuse.

————. 2003. *Evaluation of the National Youth Anti-Drug Media Campaign: 2003 Report of Findings*. By Robert Hornik, David Maklan, Diane Cadell, Carlin Henry Barmada, Lela Jacobsohn, Vani R. Henderson, Anca Romantan, Jeffrey Niederdeppe, Robert Orwin, Sanjeev Sridharan, Adam Chu, Carol Morin, Kristie Taylor, and Diane Steele. Bethesda, Md.: U.S. Department of Health and Human Services, National Institute on Drug Abuse.

————. 2004. *Secondary School Students*. Vol. 1 of *Monitoring the Future National Survey Results on Drug Use, 1975–2003*. By Lloyd D. Johnston, Patrick M. O'Malley, and Jerald G. Bachman. NIH publication no. 04-5507. Bethesda, Md.: U.S. Department of Health and Human Services, National Institute on Drug Abuse.

U.S. Department of Health and Human Services. Substance Abuse and Mental Health Services Administration. Office of Applied Studies. 1997. *Drug Abuse Warning Network Annual Medical Examiner Data 1995*. Drug Abuse Warning Network Series: D-1, DHHS publication no. (SMA) 97-3126. Rockville, Md.: U.S. Department of Health and Human Services, Substance Abuse and Mental Health Services Administration.

————. 1999. *Summary of Findings from the 1998 National Household Survey on Drug Abuse*. DHHS publication no. (SMA) 99-3328. Rockville, Md.: U.S. Department of Health and Human Services, Substance Abuse and Mental Health Services Administration.

————. 2001a. *National Estimates of Expenditures for Substance Abuse Treatment, 1997*. By Rosanna M. Coffey, Tami Mark, Edward King, Henrick Harwood, David McKusick, Jim Genuardi, Joan Dilonardo, and Mady Chalk. Rockville, Md.: U.S. Department of Health and Human Services, Substance Abuse and Mental Health Services Administration.

————. 2001b. *Summary of Findings from the 2000 National Household Survey on Drug Abuse*. NHSDA Series H-13, DHHS publication no. (SMA) 01-3549. Rockville, Md.: U.S. Department of Health and Human Services, Substance Abuse and Mental Health Services Administration.

————. 2002a. *Emergency Department Trends from the Drug Abuse Warning Network: Final Estimates 1994–2001*. DAWN Series D-21, DHHS publication no. SMA 02-3635. Rockville, Md.: U.S. Department of Health and Human Services, Substance Abuse and Mental Health Services Administration.

———. 2002b. *Substance Dependence, Abuse, and Treatment: Findings from the 2000 National Household Survey on Drug Abuse.* By Joan F. Epstein. NHSDA Series A-16, DHHS publication no. SMA 02-3642. Rockville, Md.: U.S. Department of Health and Human Services, Substance Abuse and Mental Health Services Administration.

———. 2002c. *National and State Estimates of the Drug Abuse Treatment Gap: 2000 National Household Survey on Drug Abuse.* NHSDA Series H-14, DHHS publication no. SMA 02-3640. Rockville, Md.: U.S. Department of Health and Human Services, Substance Abuse and Mental Health Services Administration.

———. 2002d. *Results from the 2001 National Household Survey on Drug Abuse: Volume III. Detailed Tables.* NHSDA Series H-18, DHHS publication no. SMA 02-3760. Rockville, Md.: U.S. Department of Health and Human Services, Substance Abuse and Mental Health Services Administration.

———. 2003. *Emergency Department Trends from the Drug Abuse Warning Network: Final Estimates 1995–2002.* DAWN Series D-21, DHHS publication no. (SMA) 03-3780. Rockville, Md.: U.S. Department of Health and Human Services, Substance Abuse and Mental Health Services Administration.

———. 2004a. *Results from the 2003 National Survey on Drug Use and Health: National Findings.* NSDUH Series H-25, DHHS publication no. SMA 04-3964. Rockville, Md.: U.S. Department of Health and Human Services, Substance Abuse and Mental Health Services Administration.

———. 2004b. *Treatment Episode Data Set (TEDS): 1992-2002. National Admissions to Substance Abuse Treatment Services.* DASIS Series: S-23, DHHS publication no. (SMA) 04-3965. Rockville, Md.: U.S. Department of Health and Human Services, Substance Abuse and Mental Health Services Administration.

U.S. Department of Justice. Bureau of Justice Statistics. 1992. Drug Enforcement and Treatment in Prisons, 1990. NCJ publication no. 134724. Washington, D.C.: U.S. Department of Justice, Bureau of Justice Statistics.

———. 1993. *Felony Sentences in State Courts, 1990.* NCJ publication no. 140186. Washington, D.C.: U.S. Department of Justice, Bureau of Justice Statistics.

———. 1999. *Substance Abuse and Treatment: State and Federal Prisoners, 1997.* NCJ publication no. 172871. Washington, D.C.: U.S. Department of Justice, Bureau of Justice Statistics.

———. 2001. *Felony Sentences in State Courts, 1998.* NCJ publication no. 190103. Washington, D.C.: U.S. Department of Justice, Bureau of Justice Statistics.

———. 2003a. *Sourcebook of Criminal Justice Statistics,* ed. Ann L. Pastore and Kathleen Maguire. http://www.albany.edu/sourcebook/ (accessed March 6, 2003).

———. 2003b. Key facts at a glance. http://www.ojp.usdoj.gov/bjs/glance/tables/corrtyptab.htm (accessed March 9, 2003).

———. 2004. Drug and Crime Facts, Drug law violations—Enforcement. http://www.ojp.usdoj.gov/bjs/dcf/tables/drugtype.htm (accessed November 19, 2004).

U.S. Department of Justice. Drug Enforcement Administration. 2002. *Drug Availability Estimates in the United States*. Report by the Drug Availability Steering Committee. Washington, D.C.: U.S. Department of Justice, Drug Enforcement Administration.

U.S. Department of Justice. Federal Bureau of Investigation. 1997. *Crime in the United States 1996*. Washington, D.C.: U.S. Department of Justice, Federal Bureau of Investigation.

———. 2004. *Crime in the United States 2003*. Washington, D.C.: U.S. Department of Justice, Federal Bureau of Investigation.

U.S. Department of Justice. Federal Bureau of Prisons. 1992. Survey of State Prisoners, 1991. http://www.ojp.usdoj.gov/bjs/abstract/sospi91.htm.

———. 2003. Quick Facts. http://www.bop.gov/fact0598.html#Drug (accessed March 9, 2003).

U.S. Department of Justice. National Institute of Justice. 1997. *Crack's Decline: Some Surprises across U.S. Cities*. By Andrew Golub and Bruce Johnson. *NIJ Research in Brief*, July. NCJ publication no.165707. http://www.ncjrs.org/pdf files/165707.pdf.

———. 2003. *Research on Drugs–Crime Linkages: The Next Generation*. By Robert MacCoun, Beau Kilmer, and Peter Reuter. http://www.ojp.usdoj.gov/ nij/drugscrime/194616.htm.

———. 2004. *Drug and Alcohol Use and Related Matters among Arrestees 2003*. By Zhiwei Zhang. http://www.ojp.usdoj.gov/nij/adam/ADAM2003.pdf (accessed January 7, 2005).

U.S. Department of Justice. National Institute of Justice. Office of Justice Programs. 1993a. *Street Gang Crime in Chicago*. By Carolyn Rebecca Block and Richard Block. Washington, D.C.: U.S. Department of Justice, National Institute of Justice.

———. 1993b. *Closing the Market: Controlling the Drug Trade in Tampa, Florida*. By David M. Kennedy. NCJ publication no. 139963. Washington, D.C.: U.S. Department of Justice, National Institute of Justice.

U.S. Department of State. Bureau for International Narcotics and Law Enforcement Affairs. 2003. *International Narcotics Control Strategy Report*. Issued March 1. Washington, D.C.: U.S. Department of State, Bureau for International Narcotics and Law Enforcement Affairs.

U.S. General Accounting Office. 1997. *Parental Substance Abuse: Implications for Children, the Child Welfare System, and Foster Care Outcomes*. GAO/T-HEHS-98-40. Washington, D.C.: U.S. General Accounting Office.

U.S. Office of National Drug Control Policy. 1989. *National Drug Control Strategy 1989*. Washington, D.C.: Executive Office of the President.

————. 1993. *State and Local Spending on Drug Control Activities*. NCJ publication no. 146683. Washington, D.C.: Executive Office of the President.

————. 1994a. *Heroin Users in New York, Chicago, and San Diego*. By Ann-Marie Rocheleau and David Boyum. Washington, D.C.: Executive Office of the President.

————. 1994b. *Guns, Drugs, and Violence in Urban Areas*. By David M. Kennedy. Washington, D.C.: Executive Office of the President.

————. 1997. *National Drug Control Strategy, 1997: FY 1998 Budget Summary*. Washington, D.C.: Executive Office of the President.

————. 2000. *What America's Users Spend on Illicit Drugs 1988–1998*. By William Rhodes, Mark Layne, Patrick Johnston, and Lynne Hozick. Washington, D.C.: Executive Office of the President.

————. 2001a. *What America's Users Spend on Illicit Drugs 1988–2000*. By William Rhodes, Mark Layne, Ann-Marie Bruen, Patrick Johnston, and Lisa Bechetti. Washington, D.C.: Executive Office of the President.

————. 2001b. *National Drug Control Strategy: 2001 Annual Report*. Washington, D.C.: Executive Office of the President.

————. 2001c. *The Economic Costs of Drug Abuse in the United States, 1992–1998*. NCJ publication no. 190636. Washington, D.C.: Executive Office of the President.

————. 2001d. *The Price of Illicit Drugs: 1981 through the Second Quarter of 2000*. Washington, D.C.: Executive Office of the President.

————. 2002a. *Drug Use Trends* (October). Washington, D.C.: Executive Office of the President.

————. 2002b. *National Drug Control Strategy: Drug Control Funding Tables*. Washington, D.C.: Executive Office of the President.

————. 2003. *National Drug Control Strategy: Update*. Washington, D.C.: Executive Office of the President.

Vega, William A., Bohdan Kolody, Jimmy Hwang, and Amanda Noble. 1993. Prevalence and Magnitude of Perinatal Substance Exposures in California. *New England Journal of Medicine* 329 (12): 850–54.

Yamaguchi, Ryoko, Lloyd Johnston, and Patrick O'Malley. 2003. Relationship between Student Illicit Drug Use and School Testing Policies. *Journal of School Health* 73 (4): 159–64.

Zaric, G. S., P. G. Barnett, and M. L. Brandeau. 2000. HIV Transmission and the Cost Effectiveness of Methadone Maintenance. *American Journal of Public Health* 90 (7): 1100–1111.

Index

Abstinence, coerced, 43, 81–82, 100–101
Additive model (drug prices), 74–75
Adolescent drug use, 6–7, 16, 17t, 21–22, 55, 67, 82, 98–99
Afghanistan, 46–47, 72, 74
African-Americans, 33, 52, 55
Aid to Families with Dependent Children, 81
AIDS, 30, 31
Alaska, 108n.2
Alcohol use, 19, 22, 29, 31, 34, 65, 105nn.19,22
Alternative crop development, 46–48
Ansliger, Harry, 5
Anti-Drug Abuse Act of 1986, 52
Anti-Drug Abuse Act of 1988, 7–8
Antidrug laws, federal, 5, 7
Arizona, 108n.2
Arrestee Drug Abuse Monitoring (ADAM) program, 18–19, 20–21
Arrestees testing positive for drug use, 18t, 19, 27
Arrests, 95
  and cocaine prices, 78t
  for drug violations, 19–20, 54–55
Asia, 46, 47, 73
Australia, 25, 98

Baltimore, 19, 65
Bennett, William, 8, 10, 27, 42

Blacks, 52, 55
Block, Carolyn and Richard, 29
"Body-packing," 107n.14
Boggs Act of 1951, 5
Bolivia, 46, 48, 72
Bourgois, Phillipe, 30
Boyum, David, 23
Brownsberger, William, 33
Budget, federal, drug control
  accuracy of, 39–42
  growth of, 37–39
  limitations as policy tool, 42–44
  overview, 36–37
Bureau of Prisons, 39–40
Bush, George H. W., 7, 8–9, 10, 16, 50
Bush, George W., 11, 49
Bushway, Shawn, 79

California, 24, 86, 108n.2
Canada, 9
Caribbean, 49, 50
Carter, Jimmy, administration, 6–7, 16
Caulkins, Jonathan, 23, 42–43, 74–76, 79, 81, 92, 95, 96
Cell-years, 7
Census Bureau, 44
Center for Substance Abuse Treatment, 61
Centers for Disease Control, 30
Certification, 48–49, 103n.4
Charleston, S. Car., 32

Retail-level enforcement, *see* Street-
level enforcement
Reuter, Peter, 3, 79
Risks, for drug dealers, 56–57,
71–72, 77–79, 95
Robert Wood Johnson Foundation, 67
Rocheleau, Ann-Marie, 23
Rubin, Robert, 87
Rydell, C. Peter, 24

Safe and Drug-Free Schools and
Communities, 40
Safe and Drug-Free Schools and
Community Act, 66
Samper government (Colombia),
48–49
Sanctions, 81–82, 98
San Diego, 18, 19, 104n.9
San Francisco, 104n.9
School-based prevention programs,
67–68, 90, 99
School budgets for drug control, 44
School district expenditures on
prevention, 106n.9
Secret Service, 38
Self-selection (bias in research),
84, 86
"Sell-and-bust," tactics, 43
Sentencing policy, 7–8, 42, 52–53, 81
reform, 95–96
state, 52, 56
Sentencing Commission, U.S., 42, 52
Sentencing Reform Act of 1984, 42
Sevigny, Eric, 81, 95
Shalala, Donna, 103n.5
Smuggling, 7, 74
Social problems, 31–32
Source-country control, 45–49, 71
effectiveness of, 72–74
recommended reform, 97
South Florida Initiative, 7
Spending, on illicit drugs, 29–30

Spraying of Mexican poppy fields, 6,
47, 73–74, 97
State
courts and drug-trafficking
convictions, 55–56
drug enforcement, 53
drug policy, 9–10
expenditures, 44–45
prisons, rise in drug commitments,
44–45
sentencing policy, 52, 56
State Department, 48
Street-level enforcement, 42–43,
53–57, 95
effectiveness, 79–81
Substance Abuse and Mental Health
Services Administration, 59, 61, 62
Supply reduction, 12–13, 17, 42–43
Supreme Court, 32

Taliban, 47
Tobacco, 9, 22, 99
Transitional Aid for Needy Families,
81–82
Treatment, 6
addiction treatment client characteristics, 59–60
effectiveness, 83–89
expenditures on, 59, 62t
managed care, 65–66
modalities, 58t
recommended reforms, 99–100
trends in spending, 61–62
Treatment Episode Data Set, 59
Treatment gap, 62–65
Treatment Outcome Prospective
Study, 88, 108n.8
Turkey, 6, 73–74, 97

Urinalysis, 19
Uniform Facility Data Set, 61,
65

About the Authors

David Boyum is an independent consultant in New York City. He has been a Robert Wood Johnson Foundation Scholar in Health Policy Research at Yale and a research fellow in the Mind/Brain/Behavior Interfaculty Initiative at Harvard. He is coauthor (with Derrick Niederman) of *What the Numbers Say: A Field Guide to Mastering Our Numerical World* (Broadway Books, 2003).

Peter Reuter is a professor in the School of Public Policy and the Department of Criminology at the University of Maryland and a senior economist in the Drug Policy Research Center at RAND. He is the author of *Disorganized Crime: The Economics of the Visible Hand* (MIT Press, 1983), and coauthor (with Robert MacCoun) of *Drug War Heresies: Learning from Other Vices, Times, and Places* (Cambridge University Press, 2001) and (with Edwin Truman) of *Chasing Dirty Money: The Fight Against Money Laundering* (Institute for International Economics, 2004). From 1999 to 2004, he was editor of the *Journal of Policy Analysis and Management*. His research focuses on international drug policy issues.